WAIT! WHAT? WE'RE GROWING!

Practical advice on how to market your orthodontic practice ... from an insider to you!

by Mel Herbinko

from Melissa Herbinko's clients ...

Whether you're just starting a practice or you own a mature practice, Mel Herbinko's accumulated knowledge, insight, and passion will be invaluable to you. Mel will actually change your life! Her manual is a must if you are serious about building and managing a large, well-coordinated practice.

- Dr. John Grady

From the moment we first met, I knew Melissa was a rockstar in the orthodontic world. Over the year that followed, she took me under her wing as I went through the process of building a start-up orthodontics practice. She graciously responded to my seemingly endless text and calls about how to plan community events, sponsorship questions, and how to spread the word about my office.

Melissa has unique skills to allow an orthodontist to create and foster relationships with referring dentists, and she's proven it in the industry for years. I'm excited for Melissa as she looks to share her knowledge with orthodontists across the nation.

- Dr. Jeffery Schaefer

This manual is essential for anyone who is even thinking about starting an orthodontics practice. Mel Herbinko teaches me something new, every single day. My confidence grows because of her insight! My start up practice is moving forward quickly because of her creative ideas on how to build meaningful relationships. She is a truly generous person to share her 27 years of experience growing one of the most successful orthodontic practices in the country. I'm so happy to have this book as a resource to pull out when I need it! The essence of Mel is building long term, TRUE relationships. Her ideas brim with tips how to do this- with young patients, parents, dental teams, members of the community, basically anyone; all of whom can be amazing referral sources.

- Dr. Manjari Kulkarni

© 2018 Melissa Herbinko.

All rights reserved. Except as permitted under the U.S. Copyright Act of 1976, no part of this book may be reproduced, scanned, transmitted or distributed in any form or by any means, or stored in any database or retrieval system, without the written permission of the publisher. Please do not participate in or encourage piracy of copyrighted materials in violation of the author's rights.

Table of contents

Prologue 1
How it all began ... and where we begin

Chapter 1 5
Roles and Responsibilities in the Orthodontic Office
... and why all of them matter when it comes to marketing

Chapter 2: 18
Measuring the size and strength of your current practice
The next step in practice growth

Chapter 3 41
Setting Goals for your Practice

Chapter 4 52
Your Marketing Toolbox
Many possibilities, and how they can work for you

Chapter 5 90
Search Engines, Optimization, Reviews and Reputation
An interview with Beth Leach of PracticeMarketer.com

Chapter 6 108
Endgame
Tracking, Testing, and Taking Care of the Team

Final Word 119
You're one of a kind. Celebrate it

Prologue
How it all began
... and where we begin!

I work every day at a single-site, multi-doctor practice in a large city in the Midwest. And sometimes when I open the office, bright and early, I find myself stopping – just for a moment! – to look around ... and remember.

Was it really twenty-seven years ago that this all began? When this was a one-doctor practice with three chairs and six team members? Because now it's *three* doctors, *fourteen chairs* and *thirty-two team members*.

How did it happen? How much did I have to do with it, and what could I have done better? And could other practice managers, patient and professional relations managers, and front-office professionals – not to mention the doctors themselves! – learn from all that we've done here?

I am asked for my opinion and advice about practice growth all the time. Sometimes I have an idea or an observation; often I don't. But this little book is my attempt to sit down and *truly* answer those questions.

What are the lessons I learned? How can what we've done here apply to orthodontic practices around the country? And what advice can I offer to orthodontic office managers and staff – people just like me, who deal with these challenges every day and want to see their practices grow and thrive, just as ours has?

My own story

Let me start with my own story, and then tell you what we're going to cover in the chapters to come.

I was nineteen years old when I was hired for my first 'real' job in the field. It wasn't my first job; in fact, the husband of one of my teachers hired me as a dental assistant while I was still in high school. He was a magnificent dentist, but I knew almost right away that I wanted a more "hands-on" experience.

A few months into that job, I saw an ad in our local paper for an orthodontic dental assistant. I called the office and they quickly set up an interview. It was only then that I recognized the name of the orthodontist who was hiring. Before I'd graduated, I had attended a career center where I'd performed a clinical rotation in this doctor's office, and even then I had been highly impressed with orthodontics.

I remember the night before my interview. I had high hopes. I had graduated from high school with high honors and my radiology license, and I already knew that this was exactly the kind of practice I wanted to join.

Maybe it was my enthusiasm; maybe it was just the perfect fit. Either way, I was hired on the spot, for $5.00 an hour and medical benefits, along with a 401K. I accepted without a second thought. Of course I did! Then I almost ran home, overjoyed, and told my mother my good news.

She was not as happy as I was. She reminded me that I had just purchased my first car, and we had done the math together; I need to make at least $5.50 an hour to cover the car payment and insurance. "You know that you make

$5.50 an hour now," she reminded me. "You're going backwards."

But I wanted this job – *really* wanted it. So I gathered my courage and phoned my new employer the next day. I explained the situation. I told him about the car. And I asked, "Is there any way you could pay me $5.50 an hour so I could make my monthly bills?" He said, "I think you might be worth that!"

Twenty-seven fabulous years, two more doctors and 26 more patient managers later … we're still working together. It certainly was worth it for *me*.

I know how very fortunate I am to have had only one orthodontic job in all this time. It's been a truly effective and sometime miraculous combination of good management, good luck, and hard work on everyone's part. Believe me, there have been plenty of "roller coaster moments" here and there along the way, but in the end I know our success is because of our teamwork. You know the old cliché: *there is no "I" in team*, and that's true in our dental practice just as it is in so many other parts of life.

Today, my official title is Professional Relations Coordinator. A lot has changed, but the heart of the practice hasn't changed at all. That's why we've been successful. And one thing is for sure: it's been an entertaining voyage. There's never been a dull day!

What we're doing, and why it should matter

My goal with *Wait! What? We're Growing!* is to summarize and expand on the lessons I've learned as the practice has grown from one doctor to three doctors and a practice that serves more than 150-175 patients a day. I'm going to start with the basics of the practice – who's involved and how they contribute – and then cover the basic process we went through and, as I've seen time and time again, every successful office needs to go through:

- Analyzing and assessing your practice, including its strengths and areas that can be improved
- Analyzing and assessing the patient population you serve
- Setting goals for practice size and growth
- Understanding the tools and tactics you can use to reach those goals
- Building a plan to reach those goals (along with a reasonable timetable)
- Making that miracle *happen*, through specific action, ongoing monitoring and assessment
- Building and maintaining morale and teamwork by working together and – believe it or not! – having fun

As you read through my notes and I give you my outlook, ask yourself if these suggestions make sense to you, and envision how they would play out in your own practice. By the time we reach the end of this journey together, I hope you'll have a clear idea of what you need to do next, a clear vision of the path in front of you and the others in your practice … and that you're ready to get started.

Let's get going!

Chapter 1
Roles and Responsibilities in the Orthodontic Office
... and why *all* of them matter when it comes to marketing

Every employee in your practice has a *role* and a *responsibility*. They're not there just to "do a job," to show up on time and supply some minimal service. They're part of the overall team, and they all have a vital role in making your practice great and "growable."

It should also go without saying – thought it doesn't! – that every position in your office should have a clearly written **job description** that is referred to during regular employee evaluations, and that is reviewed and updated for accuracy and comprehensiveness at least one or twice a year. This isn't bureaucracy or busy-work; over the years, having complete and clear job descriptions has helped me overcome personnel challenges, plan for growth, and uncover potential problems in patient relations and practice management. If you don't already have that job description, and an employee manual (whatever you might call it in your office) to go with it, or if you think there's room for major improvement, then put this book down right now and go get that done. It is an absolutely *essential* first step to making our practice as good as it can be … and ultimately helping it grow.

Cross-training is an important commitment, too. I

know this can be especially hard with small practices, but identifying who can take over when a position is vacant or someone is simply absent and a fill-in is needed is something you have to do. The job description and office manual will help with this. It gives everyone a reference guide to follow. It may take some creative thinking to establish and maintain a cross-training program, especially if you have part-time and entry-level employees, but make the practice-wide commitment and spend the time necessary to make it real. I speak from personal experience: it can make those "crisis times" when you're under pressure and short-handed so much easier to deal with.

Here is a list of the roles and responsibilities you'll find in almost every orthodontic office. The specific job titles will differ from practice to practice, and some of these functions may overlap or be handled by a single individual who has to "wear many hats," but the *functions* are fairly common.

The role of each individual position in practice growth and marketing differs. Some are obvious; some aren't. But look at it this way: every single person in your office contributes to providing excellent service to your patients and their families. And when you do that – when you fill a need for your community as vital as orthodontic care – you build a reputation that is the key, the *center*, of your growth. Establishing, keeping, and constantly growing that reputation is every employee's responsibility, and everyone benefits when everyone does an excellent job.

All that being said... here are the roles and responsibilities you always encounter in an orthodontic office:

Doctor. This role is self-explanatory, right? Without a doctor, we have no practice, and it is the responsibility of all the other team members to assist the doctor and make his or her job easier and more efficient. It is the unified role of *all* team members that allows our doctors to bring their hard-earned expertise to bear, to fully utilize their training in this specialty, so they can make the lives of their patients better.

> This is a good place to remind everyone about exactly what **orthodontics** means, and how important it is to keep that definition "top of mind."
>
> Remember, **orthodontics** is a branch of dentistry dealing *with irregularities of the teeth* (such as malocclusion) *and their correction* (as by braces, Invisalign); it is also the treatment provided by a *specialist* in orthodontics, who has received years (and continuing) education in this particular field. It's important to *always* refer to your doctors as *specialists*, and to define them as *orthodontists* in particular. They have earned that distinction!

The Greeter is the first person the patient, new or long-term, sees when they enter the office. Typically, the greeter has a great personality, is bubbly and smiling and welcoming to every single person that comes in. The greeter is the one who helps the new patient sign in for the first time and gives the office tour (in our office, that includes showing the new patients the tooth-brushing room they can use). The purpose is to make the new patient super-comfortable, so in the future they're already familiar with where they're going and what they can expect. When the short "intro" is complete, the Greeter hands off the new patient to...

The Records Coordinator. In almost all cases, the new patient has already filled out most of the necessary forms and given general medical history (we talk about that more in a bit). But the Records Coordinator makes sure that's all done, and then move on to getting the rest of what's needed before the examination, diagnosis, and treatment can begin. They do all the impression, X-rays, and digital scans. They complete the "profile" of the patient, and then introduce them to ...

Treatment Coordinator. The TC is the one who knows what the patient is going to need, and what the practice can offer to them. They have a pretty good idea of what the doctor is going to propose when it comes to bites, procedures, skeletal discrepancies, available tools and technologies, etc. It's the TC's expertise that allows the doctor to spend only a few minutes with the patient on this first visit (in our practice, it's scheduled as no more than nine to thirteen minutes; yours may have different ranges). This initial meeting with the patient, even though it may only be a single encounter, is as important to establishing expectations and a quality experience as the continuing relationship that the Doctor and the Patient Manager create. It's another old cliché that turns out to be true: it's all about first impressions (literally!).

Patient Manager. The title may have changed over the years (we used to call them *orthodontic dental assistants*), but the job itself is more important than ever. Bottom line: the Patient Manager's job is to *make the patient feel they are important.* It's as simple (and difficult!) as that. The PM works with the individual patient from start to finish – the same Patient Manager, every time they visit (though obviously the patient may have a different PM for different procedures or challenges over the years). Even when the PM is on vacation or otherwise unavailable, it's important to manage patient schedules *around* those absences, to establish a consistent one-on-one relationship that is not interrupted. PM's are usually assigned after the initial consultation, and continue through

What about the Office Manager?

I am often asked, "What's the role of the office manager at your practice, and in orthodontic practices in general?"

In fact, we do have an office manager ... but that may change in the future. Over the years, we've come to think that not every office needs one.

It's absolutely important that everyone in the office has someone in charge – someone to report to – and that everyone involved is clear on who their "go-to person" is. For example, the Patient Manager probably has a Senior Patient Manager who knows what the PM is doing on a day-to-day, patient-by-patient basis. The Greeter and Scheduling Coordinator report to the Clinical Coordinator; the Professional Relations Coordinator reports directly to the doctor (though we try to keep the number that do report to the doctor directly to a manageable number).

In this structure, the classic "office manager" role is a little obsolete. An OM becomes a middleman, and the OM's involvement just makes the chain of command longer. Often the OM is put in the position of simply saying, "Go ask the doctor," which doesn't do anyone any good. So it's worth looking at the command structure in your office – the various roles your people have taken on and who they report to – and then asking yourself (and each other), "Is this really the best way to do things?" After all, everyone's goal in the office should be to make things run more smoothly, not slow things down. The question is ... does an Office Manager help you reach that goal?

comprehensive treatment. They do all the work: putting the brackets or appliances on, answering questions, making the follow-up calls. They are as much the "face of the practice" to individual patients as the doctor.

Financial/insurance Coordinator. Money matters – to *everyone*, regardless of their socioeconomic level, available cash, current insurance, or family pressures. That's why the work of the financial coordinator is so important to your practice and its reputation. The Coordinator will sit with the patient early on and discuss all the options that are available – insurance (and its limitations), financing, acceptance of credit cards, discounts when patients can pay in full, acceptance (or non-acceptance) of state-funded insurance.

At the practice where I work, we've made the corporate decision that all children in our community deserve quality orthodontic care, no matter where they come from. It can make a difference in their lives that will literally last a lifetime, especially when their challenges can be addressed at the age of eight or nine rather than 30. We work very hard to find financing options that can work for every child, and we talk about that openly and regularly. How that actually happens is the responsibility of the Finance/Insurance Coordinator … and our continuing success in providing that service is one of the keystones of our reputation in the community. It's paid us back a hundred times over.

Having a Coordinator who is not only creative, clever, informed and patient, but who can *relate* to patients – who is a good talker *and* a good listener, who can explore and explain difficult subjects (and financial discussions are almost always difficult!) – is a major asset to a growing practice. *Now* is a good time to look at your Coordinator's skills, not only as an insurance and financing expert, but at his or her person-to-person skills, and find ways to help them improve those skills even more through seminars, training, and coaching. It's another investment that always pays off. You expect a TC or PM to be a "people person." You should expect and rely on your Finance/Insurance Coordinator to be the same!

Scheduling Coordinator. Time is money ... and time is often happiness as well. The Scheduling Coordinator is the person responsible for "making the trains run on time": scheduling appointments and no-shows, handling any phone calls that come in to confirm or change appointments, and every maddening variation on that theme. Every office has one and we all need them; it is so important to treat them well and give them the tools they need. For example, a Scheduler deserves to have proper scripting when taking a new patient phone call (here again: first impressions are everything!).

We've even developed a "New Patient Phone Slip" for our Schedulers. The slip includes important details to ensure that all the important patient information we need is captured, recorded, and entered on the patient chart from the very beginning, so there's no confusion or need to repeat the process at any point. Among the most important data points (and we'll talk more about this later) is *how the patient found out about our practice*. In fact, we consider the referral source as the most important part of taking that new patient phone call, second only to the concern that brought the patient into the office in the first place. Communication skills are essential here, of course, but so is providing the Scheduler with the tools to get it right (and make it easy to get it right) every time.

Clinical Coordinator. The Clinical Coordinator sits at the center of the web (and sometimes the hurricane) that is a busy clinic. The Coordinator knows where the doctors, Patient Managers, and other staff are at all times – where each of them is going, when, and how long they'll be there. They greet the patients as they come in the door and make sure the Greeter is there to get this started; they make those patients feel comfortable and show them that everything is under control, and they're dedicated to the idea of getting the patients out of the waiting room and into the chair in the shortest possible time. A good Clinical Coordinator is worth his or her weight in gold – almost literally – and deserves ongoing praise, training, improvement, and reward.

Professional Relations Coordinator. That's me! At the practice where I am the Coordinator, I work with all the referring offices, create and execute our marketing efforts, find new marketing opportunities, and stage the community events that bring new patients in the door, as well as get existing patients coming back for more. For me, about sixty percent of my time is spent on marketing and the remainder on the expansion, care and feeding of our referrals network, a hugely important part of our plan and something we'll talk about at length later on. As our population changes in size and shape, as our services expand and opportunities evolve, investing in a full-time Professional Relations Coordinator has turned out to be a great financial decision, and one that continues to pay off.

Human Resources. Even the pure "support" staff positions play a vital role in marketing. Our HR person is our reliable "go to" for everything to do with payroll, taxes, and 401(K) issues. This is the desk that makes sure the bills get paid, and that our own insurance is the best possible for the price (almost a full time job in itself!). Having a steady, consistent human resource manager who makes sure the paychecks come on time and the lights stay on gives every employee a sense of confidence and a positive attitude that can't be faked. That translates into a better experience for patients and employees alike. It's not to be underestimated.

Lab Technician. Many multi-doctor offices have invested in an in-office lab and lab tech as well. It's a major step, it's true, but I can tell you that when it comes to my practice, there have been huge advantages to having in-house help. When patients get their braces off, they get their retainers the same day; appliances take only a week or two, so there are no long wait-times and rarely a need to "send things out." Here again, that fast, personalized service is something we talk about often, and that patients themselves brag about to friends and family, which in turn supply a steady stream of referral and repeat business. This is exactly why *everyone* in the practice, from the people who work in the front office to everyone who is "behind the scenes," is an important part of marketing. They all provide excellent service and change patient lives for the better. When they do that consistently and creatively, word gets out … and "word of mouth" is the single greatest force in practice growth, bar none.

Aligner Specialist. Whether your specialist is full-time, part-time, or "on call," there's a great advantage to having a professional whose entire focus is on the constantly evolving technology of aligners like Invisalign, Orchestrate, and all the others. Having an Aligner Specialist makes you a trusted source of information for everyone – the place with an expert in the field on staff that everyone can turn to. It can make a big difference.

IT Manager. My multi-doctor practice is large enough that having a full-time IT Manager, and for us that makes good sense. Everything in the office – literally every bit of data, every medical record, every image – is digitized, and almost nothing is more important than keeping those systems secure and running smoothly. Why does this matter for practice marketing? Remember the last time you went to your bank or gas station, or even your favorite restaurant, and couldn't get what you wanted because "the computers are down"? How did that make you feel … and how did it affect your recommendations of that bank or store or eatery? The same applies to an orthodontic practice. The last thing you want is a rep for being disorganized or unreliable, and even a single instance of a "broken" IT or internet system can do damage. Whether your IT support is part-time, contracted, or full-time, it's a vital part of the "invisible machine" that makes a successful office.

Now: Make a Map

Seriously. Think about these roles and responsibilities – regardless of the titles you may use – and how they are handled in your own office. Take as much time as you need to actually draw out a diagram – a map, really – of who does what, and how they're backed up (assuming they are).

Understanding how your practice works at the operational level will help you understand what your strengths really are – what you can emphasize, even brag about, as you build an effective message to convey to your community. Maybe you have a phenomenal Clinical Coordinator that everyone loves. You can talk about that. Maybe you're the only orthodontic practice in town with its own in-house lab, or a website everyone talks about, or an above-average commitment to financing for people in need. Whatever it is, understanding your office as it exists today will help you improve it in the future, and present opportunities for you to brag about it, *present* it, to the public. Those are important insights to have as we move on to the next part of the process: measuring and understanding the size, strength, and opportunities of your practice and your patient population.

Chapter 2
Measuring the size and strength of your current practice
The next step in practice growth

When you begin a new journey, the first step is always *understanding where you're starting from*. This chapter is about exactly that: getting a clear, sharp, and *complete* picture of your orthodontic practice as it exists right now: its strengths and weaknesses, the population it serves, and its place in your community. Only when you measure and appreciate your practice's unique characteristics can you make a workable and effective plan to improve and grow.

All the news won't be good. You'll discover 'blank spots' and areas for development. But it's vitally important to get a clear picture of where you are before you even begin.

So let's go over the list of what you need to know.

First: describe your practice (present and future)

You've already begun this process by listing all the office staff's roles and mapping your structure. But there's more to understanding your practice. Take some time to think about and answer the following questions ...

Do you have any 'specialties' you're known for? Whether you've marketed them effectively or not ... are there any aspects of the practice that are well known in your community? You could be "the pediatric orthodontist," who's great with kids. You could be the local expert on working with the elderly, or with the obese, or in accident reconstruction. As an example: at my practice, we are known for our expertise in airway obstruction and sleep apnea. We receive referrals from primary care providers and sleep specialists to help with appliances and procedures that can address these issues. We have only recently begun to think about an advertising or marketing campaign that 'spreads the word' about that specific focus; maybe your office has some already existing specialty that deserves to be discussed and emphasized as well.

How good (or not so good) is your reputation in your community? This is an entirely subjective measurement, and ties into the "competitive analysis" and "reputation management" issues we will discuss later, but it's worth looking into here in a general way.

Start by asking your own staff. Everyone you work with has a general sense of how well-regarded your office is – with patients, with other professionals, in the community at large. As you're talking with your team members, ask them to give you an estimate of their own practice's reputation with those 'outside' groups on a simple scale of 1 to 10. Make it clear that their response is entirely confidential, and that there will be no argument or retaliation; you're just looking for a quick opinion. You will probably find that your staff's assessments 'cluster' around one or two numbers, and knowing what your own staff thinks of your reputation can be valuable as you try to build a better "rep" and improve office morale.

Does anyone on the team stand out in the community, or is particularly well-known? It is sometimes easy to forget that team members have lives outside of the office ... and their activities with their families and the community at large can actually be important to the practice. Maybe one of your PM's is a leader in their church; maybe your Finance Manager is an officer in the local Chamber of Commerce, or your Greeter is a volunteer at the local animal shelter. There may be opportunities for growth, recognition, or simply to help others in your community, and there may be 'hidden' connections already in place, just waiting to be discovered. So ask as you go: What other organizations or community commitments do you or members of your team have?

Are there non-profit organizations that you consistently support? Your doctors and office leadership probably already have non-profits or charitable organizations they know, work with, and support. As you build a more detailed marketing plan for the future, it's valuable to know what those organizations or general areas of interest are, and to spend some time thinking how you can build or strengthen those ties in the future in an organized and directed way.

Think about your practice's future. What specialties or emphases would your dental team like to develop or publicize? This highly subjective process of "quality measurement" isn't just about the present; it's about the future as well. Your doctors or other professional staff may have recently discovered a specialty or field of study that interests them; they may be beginning training or are midway through a continuing education or certification process that could change your practice in the near or far future. Ask about this. Help make a plan for that professional and practice development. There may be opportunities for growth or change in practice marketing that will benefit everyone, and it's worth knowing and supporting these future goals in the present.

… and once you've completed that list, talk with your doctor and key members of your support team to make sure everyone agrees. You may find that other members of the office have insights of their own, and may even offer contradictory ideas about your current specialties and future potential. There's a lot of important information to be gained with a simple (if sometimes challenging!) set of conversations.

Once you've created a clear idea of your office and how it works …

Next: Describe your community

Your office has a place in the community, simply by virtue of being there. And the majority of your patient population comes from the neighborhoods that immediately surround your office (in fact, studies show that as much as 80% of your patients live and/or work within a ten-mile radius or less, depending on how dense the community might be.) So it's worth knowing as much as you can about that community; that knowledge can inform your decision-making from the very beginning.

The data points to gather include:

> Geography and demographics. Every community has a "personality" based on its history, geography and demographics. Maybe your office is in a suburb that's filled with growing families and young children; maybe it's a college town or near a retirement community. It may be ethnically diverse or homogeneous, or there may be one or more predominant ethnic groups nearby.
>
> Chances are you already know this – you live there or nearby, after all! – but the simple act of summarizing that 'vision' of your community can be informative. Here again, your view and the view of your doctors and team members may be different, and that's worth knowing too. There may be potential 'pockets' within the community that you're not effectively engaging, and taking some time to think about the people around you can be beneficial.
>
> Even geography matters. Are you part of or near a larger city? Are you a small town, fairly isolated from other communities (and other practices) by distance? Is weather a factor for patients (and for staff) even part of the year?

This doesn't require extensive research or a lot of statistics, but it does require some attention and thought. It is part of the process of literally knowing where you are before you begin your journey.

As an example: My 'home' practice is in the suburbs, about 15 miles outside a major Midwest urban center. We know that people prefer to stay local for their services, but the wider choices and larger diversity of the "big city" are literally just down the road. That's why we emphasize our local commitment so strongly. That's something for you to consider, too.

Major local annual or seasonal events. Almost every community has a local harvest festival, or annual music festival, or holiday parade – often a whole collection of them. As you'll see when we discuss the value of marketing at some of these events, it's good to know *in advance* when those 'big days' are, and how early you need to plan to be part of them. You can build this list by simply 'asking around' the office to make sure you've included all the obvious ones. Everybody already knows!

Schools, colleges, trade schools. Depending on your community's demographics and your own practice characteristics, educational institutions, from pre-schools to post-graduate schools, can be rich sources of new patients and marketing opportunities. In some communities, there are a few key schools. In others there are an almost endless variety. Begin the list with the most obvious … then do a bit of digging and be sure to add trade schools, after-school programs, and extended learning groups. Just a list with basic contact information may spark some ideas and encourage obvious connections.

Important or powerful non-profits, churches, and charities. Every community has a wide range of church and non-profit organizations already hard at work – many of them decades old. Trying to keep a complete list of those could be a full-time job in itself. But in every community, a handful of those organizations are significant *influencers*, places where relatively large numbers of potential patients are involved, and whose opinions and allies are respected and responded to. So choose an arbitrary number – ten, a dozen, no more than fifteen – and make a list of the 'big players' in town. Don't try to be complete about this one; if you do, you could easily feel overwhelmed. But for the big ones that really matter, gather the basic contact information, and add no more than a sentence or two describing each. Here, too, you may want to ask your staff if they have any to add or edit, and discovering any 'built-in' connections to these groups can be very beneficial. It's a list that needs to be revisited and updated a couple of times a year. Things change, and sometimes can change to your advantage.

Sports and recreational venues. What are the most popular sports in your community? The most popular teams? And this obviously includes local, even high school competitions. Are there any major sporting events held in the area (including annual events, like marathons or bike races)? What sponsorships or community-participation availabilities are there that you might want to consider? Especially when it comes to orthodontic devices and protections, sports and recreational issues can be very important … and getting involved with local teams, fan organizations, and venues can provide major 'gateways' for your practice.

Finally, let's talk about the single most important aspect of understanding your community:

Competitive Analysis:
Awareness, Attitude, Approach

It's absolutely vital that you know as much as you can about the other orthodontic and dental practices in your vicinity, including their specialties and what their overall strengths and reputations are.

It's not particularly healthy or productive to look at competitors as enemies, or that you're in some kind of 'war' with your colleagues. This is not a battle, but it *is* a competition, and it's good to know what choices are available to your current and potential patients, and understand the reasons why they might choose a practice other than yours.

There's no question, orthodontics has become much more competitive in recent years. Even in my own relatively small community, there are a lot of competitors – and not just other orthodontists. Dentists have begun to 'dabble' in our field, offering Invisalign and similar services. And the number of single- and multiple-location orthodontic offices, where a single doctor may have three or four storefront offices in different, distributed communities, has virtually exploded in the last few years.

Defining 'weaknesses' also points out opportunities.

There are other ways that competitive analysis doesn't have to be threatening or depressing. Just as "everybody's doing it" became "we are specialists," competitive analysis can point out new opportunities for defining yourself and growing.

For example, I'm part of a large practice – a single location with three doctors, working full time (and then some!). Our competitive analysis showed us that we are unique in our community in this way; all our direct competitors in the area have a single doctor in one office or a number of small regional offices for a single doctor. At first, this might look as if we are at a disadvantage – we could be seen as less convenient for some potential patients. But then we realized that if a patient has an orthodontic emergency, and their orthodontist at another practice is in a different regional office that day, they may have to drive an hour or an hour and a half to get the treatment they need. "Not with us," we pointed out. "We're right here, nearby, all the time, with a full staff on site." That's an advantage, and we talk about it often. It's an important thing for consumers to know when they're shopping, and we always tell them that. And only competitive analysis gave us that awareness and ability to respond.

It's a fact of modern life for practice marketing: every parent, every patient, is "shopping" for orthodontic treatment, visiting multiple web sites, checking Yelp, asking friends and other family members. Knowing your competition is an essential response to that reality. You have to know who the other orthodontists and dentists in your area are, what they're offering, and why what *you* offer is unique and superior. But if you don't look around, and see what other options are available to them, you won't know what to point out – what to brag about. As much as you might like to, you can't avoid the other professionals in town. You have to know who they are and what the community wants before you start.

How to view and work with your competitors.

As strange as it may sound to some people, you

need to be friends with your competitors. Yes, they *are* competitors, and you're all working hard to acquire and keep your patients … but keep in mind, there are enough crooked teeth to go around. In the long run, you need to work together, not against each other.

And you certainly can't ignore what others are doing. As an example: we noticed some time ago that there were a number of weekend "festivals," community events, that were very popular with the families in our community – especially with families with young kids, who were at the center of our target market. You know the events: music and 'street' performers, food and games. No one thought about events like this as an opportunity for an orthodontist, but we decided to take a chance: we invested in a booth there, offered prizes and passed out brochures, and ended up having a terrific (and profitable) time.

No other orthodontic or dental practice in our area had ever done that … but now, just a few years later, *five other local practices* are regular participants in that event and others like it, just like we are. They were smart: they were watching their competition, saw something new that worked, and made it their own. We've done the same in other areas. So should you.

Now: Learn All You Can About Your Current Patient Population

Now you know a lot about your own practice and the people you work with, and you have a good idea of the community that you're a part of. Now let's get to the most important group of all: your patient population.

Who are they? Why do they come to you, and what do they want and need most? Knowing about your patients is hugely important, and the more you know, the better you can serve them … and the more you can grow.

Your patient management software will be a big help here. Asking direct questions of the patients you already have and the new ones who come to you is equally helpful, and we'll talk about how to do that later on in this chapter. You'll probably find that you already know the answers to many of these questions; they just need to be confirmed and pulled together as part of the planning process. And you might get some surprises, too.

Here are just some of the things you'll want to learn:

Number of patients. This is more than just a count of your entire patient base – though that number is informative all by itself. There's much more to it.

Use your practice management software to tell you:

- The number of open cases you have at the moment

- How many cases you've taken on *and completed* in the last year

- How many of those cases were new (that is, patients who were visiting for the first time) and how many were continuing patients from earlier work

Each one of these numbers has an important role; we'll see why.

The age range of your patients. In our office, as in most practices, we have at least a few patients from every age group. Our youngest patient at the moment is four years old; our oldest is past seventy. But the *percentages* are what matter. Our software tells us that our practice is about 60% children (in our practice, we define that is "before and during puberty") and about 40% are adults. Your percentages may be entirely different. Remember, too, that "adult" can cover a wide range of people with entirely different issues, so breaking it down further – at least into 21 years old to 55 versus 55+ – may be of use too.

Why is this important? Because different age groups use different products and procedures and respond to different kinds of marketing (as we will explore later). Children don't make their own decisions, of course, but parents – especially mothers – do, and they will have an entirely different set of media habits and decision-making processes than other groups, like senior citizen, which may be different, in turn, than the decision-making process of a single adult who's making a decision only for themselves. So knowing how much of your practice falls into these very different groups is extremely helpful.

Gender. How many of your current patient base is

female, and how much is male? It's worth making note of this "gender split" among patients who are children, teens, and adults, too. This can affect everything from the kinds of media you choose for marketing and advertising to the kinds of "before and after" pictures you post. It's also interesting and helpful to note the change in those percentages over time. In our own practice, the split is about 50/50, but we've also noticed that the number of boys and adult males has grown as a percentage over the last few years. So we're experimenting with the idea of reaching out even more to adult men, and featuring as many young boys and young girls in our ads for pediatric services – a definite change in recent years.

Patient lifetime. It's very important to realize that most of your patients *keep coming back*. They rarely come to the office for just one procedure, never to be seen again. They often return for follow-ups and additional procedures and services. (They are also a rich referral source, but we'll talk about that later.) And of course a single procedure involves a number of visits that can easily last six months or more. Each visit is another opportunity for marketing.

We tend to categorize most of our procedures into early treatment and comprehensive treatment. Phase 1 is just early treatment, involving things like upper and lower expanders, upper and lowers braces, space maintainers, thumb cribs for children who suck their thumbs, and more. Comprehensive treatment includes adult tooth-straightening procedures like braces, Invisalign, lingual braces, orthognathic surgery, etc.

Knowing how many of your current patient base is in Phase 1 and how many are in Phase 2 can change the focus and emphasis of marketing. You need to know what kind of challenges your patients are facing, and how to help them make smart decisions as they come to those critical moments.

You can predict, or at least project, when those critical moments will occur. Most orthodontic procedures last six to eight weeks; we "check in" with our young patients who had their early (Phase 1) treatment every seven to eight months, until all their baby teeth have fallen out and all their adult teeth have come in. That's when we investigate their need or interest in a second phase of treatment (Invisalign, ceramic braces, full cosmetic procedures, or other approaches). We have a different timetable for adults and their comprehensive treatment, but no more than a few months go by without contact – not for any of our active cases. We consider this a long-term, even lifelong, relationship.

We rarely get any negative reaction from our patients when we call to check in or remind them about follow-up appointments. After all, they have already invested a lot of time and money in us to be perfectionists for them, and that doesn't stop with the successful completion of that first (or second, or third) procedure. So we never feel bad or "uninvited." If the Phase 1 patient doesn't reach out to us, we follow up to them. Our management system, like almost all patient management systems on the market, has a calendar function and "recall" system that makes these follow-ups simple and smart. Ask yourself: does your practice do the same? Systematically and automatically?

Family involvement *(more than one patient per household)*. This is one of the most important, and often most under-appreciated aspects of your patient population. Obviously, your younger patients are being brought in by a parent; often those children have brothers and sisters, younger or older, who are potential patients. And the *parents themselves* are potential patients as well. Take a look at your current patient base and see what percentage of them have siblings or multiple generations who also have open cases. Ask yourself: can that percentage be larger? Are there opportunities here that are being left "on the table"?

Patient media preferences and habits. One final, important thing to learn about each patient is: *how did they find out about your office in the first place?*

We use an actual form – a "New Patient Slip" – to ask that the first time the patient calls in, and that's very helpful. But there can be more. Often the new patient may not remember, or may *think* they first heard about us from a friend or on social media, but don't really recall. So asking directly and recording that information is important ... but beyond that, learning about that patients' overall *media habits* – how they get their information in general, what newspapers they read, radio stations they listen to, websites they visit, social media they use – can be very important as you build specific tactics for marketing and advertising.

Some things we already know:

- Local community web sites help many people make decisions about dental and orthodontic care (and health care in general, for that matter), especially parents and younger adults. Yelp and other "review" and recommendation sites carry a lot of influence.
- Print advertising has lost much of its impact (remember Yellow Pages?), and newspaper circulation, even local newspapers, is down. But print advertising in event programs, special publications, and community guides may still be worthwhile.

- Having well-made and effective print ads ready and up-to-date is important, but very few practices rely on them the way they used to.
- More than anything else, social media matters. *Facebook is huge.* Does your practice have a Facebook page, and who is responsible for keeping it current and interesting with new content? How good a job are they doing? Do you have Twitter or Instagram accounts as well? Should you? (and the answer isn't always "yes." Once again, it depends on your patient population's overall media preferences and habits.) The most important point is that it's not just Facebook anymore. Depending on your practice and patient base, it's *Facebook and ...* and it's time to fill in that blank, and revisit that question on a regular basis.

A word about reputation management

Generally speaking, the more local community pages you're on, the better for the practice. Parents and young professionals look at them regularly and give them a lot of weight. You should keep an eye on the most active and influential community pages you know, and when someone adds a recommendation or a review on there, it's worth responding, to show how active and engaged the practice really is.

Even negative reviews or comments can be valuable, both as "life lessons" for the practice and as opportunities to learn and make amends. A response like "Thank you; we weren't aware of that. We'll address it" can go a long way towards repairing or averting any permanent damage by taking responsibility and showing your concern. If and when this "reputation management" process becomes too time-consuming and complex, it may be time to bring in the professionals to handle it for you, and there are a few good ones out there. The most important thing, however, is not to let it get away from you. Better to ask for help than to give up. Your online reputation is powerful and important, and becoming more important every day.

We talk much more about social media, reviews, and reputation management in Chapter 5. Keep reading!

How did you find all this out?

This is a lot of information and it may take some time and dedication to gather it all. But an effective marketing plan and the actual growth of your practice requires a good, solid set of facts (and some figures!) to build on.

You have three powerful tools available to you:

- Your patient management software
- Your staff
- Your patient base

Getting the parents to take care of themselves

This is an important tactic – important enough to talk about in greater detail. Almost every day, I encounter a Mom (or, more rarely, a Dad) who's sitting in the waiting room as his or her child has treatment. I strike up a conversation, and they often say something like, "Yes; I wish I'd had braces when I was a kid." From previous experience, I know that this is the best moment to say, "Well, this is a great time to get started. In fact, you and your children can do it together; you can even combine appointments and make it super-convenient." This gets them thinking. Then I offer to do a *free* digital scan, right then and there, which includes a simulation of how they'll look before and after their own treatment, and that's the ticket they need to see, to show them what their teeth would look like, what can be done with braces or Invisalign or other treatments. At that point, far more often than not, it's straight to, "Okay, sign me up. That's a no-brainer."

This approach is simple, fast, and amazingly effective. At my home practice, our conversion rate, from conversation to case, is more than 80%. That's right: about 8 out of 10 start treatment that day!

If you are lucky enough to have someone in your office who can take this on, it's well worth trying. In fact, it's worth finding or cultivating someone who

> would be good at it and giving them a "new patient" bonus for every success. It can expand the practice, multiply the number of procedure and patients without going outside the office itself, simply by addressing the (only slightly hidden) needs of the entire family you're already serving.

The patient management software you already have is almost certainly able to give you a lot of the information you need about the number of patients, gender, age, procedures and return visits. If not, it's time to consider new software. If it is capable of doing all this, and you're not sure how to draw it out, a thorough Google search for answers or a call to the company might be necessary. Before you spend a lot of time trying to dredge though all the files yourself, ask for a bit of help.

Your staff. You may be surprised (though you shouldn't be!) at how much your staff already knows. Having a series of *short* meetings, asking for specific information and insight about everything from reputation to patient behavior to each staff member's own activities and goals is another great investment with potentially big pay-off. Some practices have had success with weekend retreats; others use a series of lunchtime meetings or after-hours get-togethers. Some have even used confidential questionnaires (though I have found face-to-face discussions are better than written surveys, even when you're talking about sensitive subjects). As you're building this "portrait" of your practice, your community, and your patient base, don't underestimate the importance of your staff … or what they already know.

The patient base itself. You don't get if you don't ask ... and in this case, directly asking your patients for information – about everything from media habits to referrals – is super-important.

Do you have a questionnaire that your intake people use when patients call? It's a very valuable tool. We call ours a "New Patient Slip," and it includes basic questions about where they are, who referred them, their insurance (and that information may affect when they get the appointment). It's not a long or elaborate script, but we use it *every time* a new patient calls. It's not the medical information – that's handled separate (see below) – but it gets information that's just as important as medical data.

That first phone call also works directly with our web site. Before we hang up, we ask the new patient to go to the site – we have a simple URL so it's easy to do – and we ask them to fill out their medical information there, rather than over the phone or waiting until they come into their appointment. There are a couple of great reasons for this: (1) long visits to the web site improve our search engine optimization numbers (SEO), and help us appear higher up on the results in Google searches and elsewhere, and (2) We get more accurate responses than we do from phone questionnaires or in-office forms. When new patient first visit the office, they're often already stressed; they may rush through the forms, or not have every bit of information they should at their fingertips. If they're at home and doing it at their own pace, we get more accurate data, and we're able to act on it in advance of that first appointment, so by the time they come into the office, everything is ready:

there are no more forms to fill out, no insurance issues to struggle with. They simply sign in on the computer and they're taken on their tour: the appointment begins. Our goal is to make the first visit as smooth and friendly as possible, with absolutely no paperwork. *None.* And a partnership of phone calls and the web site has made that possible.

We've included the "New Patient Slip" that our intake people use on the next page. It may not suit your practice perfectly, so feel free to come up with your own version. But the process of using that first phone call and your well-made web site to "lock up" a new patient and learn all you can is a time-tested tactic that attracts *and keeps* new patients. And what you learn about them along the way is hugely helpful.

Here's our "New Patient Phone Slip"

NEW PATIENT PHONE SLIP

ID # _____   APPOINTMENT DATE: _____

Today's Date: _____

Patient's Name: _____

D.O.B.: _____   AGE: _____

Parent's Name(s): _____ E-mail: _____

Address: _____ City: _____ Zip: _____

Cell: (412 724) _____   Receive Texts? Y   N   Phone #2: (412 724) _____

Has any family member been a patient here? _____

Patient's Dentist: _____   Panorex: Y (dated: __/__/____) N

Referred by: _____

Allergies: _____   NONE

Does patient have any oral habits?   Bite Nails   Grinds Teeth   Sucks Thumb   NONE

Is there anything else we should know for the consultation?

_____

_____

Has the patient had previous ortho treatment?   Y   N

Does patient have government insurance? UPMC for You/ Kids/ Children,   Gateway,   United Healthcare Community Plan

Insurance Company Name/Phone Number: _____

Name of Policy Holder: _____   B. Date: _____

Social Security # OR ID # of Policy Holder: _____

Policy Holder's Employer: _____

Do you wish to have any other children seen at this time for an orthodontic consultation?:   Y   N

Doctor Preference: JMG   DEK   MCG   NONE

Do you know where the office is located?   Y   N

    Mail form   Gave form   Download form   In Office   Consult Phone call Taker:
                                                                                                                                _____

Chapter 3
Setting Goals for Your Practice

Congratulations! You've invested a lot of time, energy, and thought in learning about your own practice, your team, your community, and your current patient population. Now it's time to pull that all together to set some goals and make a plan.

Over the years, I've found that there are some good 'rules of thumb' to keep in mind when you're setting goals for the practice.

- **They should be specific.** Not just "get bigger" or "make more money," but "increase new patients by 10%" or "attend five more community events in the next twelve months." Don't be afraid of numbers or percentages, just be clear so you can make an honest measurement and assessment along the way.

- **They should be achievable.** Of course we all like to dream. We'd all love the practice to be wildly successful with no additional effort on anyone's part. But we also know that's just not how things work in the real world. So as you set your goals, be honest with yourself and your team and set goals for your practice that you really believe can actually be achieved. Not "if you're lucky," or "if everything goes perfectly," but ones that you believe you can reach with hard work and focus. It's a time to be positive, yes, but remember that setting the bar *too* high can actually de-motivate your team.

- **There should only be a few.** It's a temptation to set a lot of goals: number of patients, monthly revenue, number of procedures, number of events, etc. etc. But it can easily become impossible to keep track – or even remember! – A long, long list of goals (even specific ones). In the first rounds, look at everything and set as many goals as you like. But in the final discussions, narrow that list down to the *really* important ones. Generally I've found no less than three but no more than five is manageable; fewer than three may mean you're not reaching high enough; six or more may mean you've made things a little too complicated and tough to follow.

- **Work to get 'buy-in' for everyone on the team.** Even the best set of short, specific, achievable goals can fall on deaf ears if they're just 'plopped' in front of team members in a memo or at a team meeting, without their involvement or participation. We'll talk a bit more about how to achieve this, but it's worth mentioning right up front: these are *team* goals, *whole-practice* goals, not just words or numbers on a paper or in a report. And everyone should be a part of making that list and achieving it (as well as share in the rewards).

Setting goals is absolutely necessary, of course, but the final document or report or format to present these goals can (and should) be tailored to your practice and the personality of your office. Maybe they're listed on a single sheet and posted in the break room; maybe they're reviewed (quickly and accurately) in a monthly or quarterly team meeting. Maybe there are drawings of "thermometers" on white boards in the staff lounge, so everyone can see how they're progressing towards the goal. Give some thought to how you get *and keep* people engaged in goal-setting and goal-achieving, and find ways to encourage them rather than make them feel threatened or 'under the gun.'

So I'll leave the shape and 'look' of that final document to you and your team. Instead, let's talk about the process of setting goals instead.

First: look at your recent past

When it comes to analysis of your practice's recent performance, the days of spreadsheets and hand-counting are long gone. The software you use to schedule and bill your patients can also supply you with very valuable reports about the numbers of patients, the number of new patients, the types of procedures, the number of visits, and (of course!) revenue. First time around, you may want to pull *all* of those reports, but you'll quickly learn which ones really matter and which ones don't.

And remember all those tracking codes we talked about, for every call-in and promotion? This is when that information – hand-collated or stored in the system

– becomes so important. Even as you're looking at patient and procedure data, you should also be looking at which promotions, and which *kinds* of promotions, paid off in the best way. And of course "paid off" is a relative term. We'll talk about ROI, or "Return on Investment," below, but keep in mind that the "return" for *some* promotions is "payment" in good will in the community, general visibility for the practice, and morale-building for your team. These are all important factors, alongside dollars and sense.

By the end of your seasonal survey of the past, you should have a pretty good idea of what's worked well, what needs improvement and what should be de-emphasized or even removed from your plans for the future. The lesson is: learn from your past activities, and build on that foundation.

Choose (and then refine) your 'goalposts'

Now that you've looked at all those reports, do a little 'editing.' Work out which of these data-points really matter the most to your doctors and your team. In our practice, we've found that we look at the *types of procedures* with the same sharp focus as *number of patients*, and that we look at *returning patients* (and family members) with the same level of detail as *new patients*. And of course we're always taking stock of how well *professional referrals* are going.

All together, we have about half a dozen "metrics" that we watch, and we've succeeded and boiling those down to four general categories. We call these the "goalposts," and your goalposts may be different than ours – *should* be different, in fact, because you're part of your own practice with its own strengths, market characteristics and personal goals. But it's important for all practices to go through the process of looking at *all* the metrics and making some decisions about what to watch most closely. And the final list of metrics should be relatively short and easy to pull together and understand. (Not always an easy task!)

Focus on ROI rather than budget

I'm often asked if the practice I'm a part of has a marketing budget that gets approved every year or every half. Oddly, the answer is "no." That doesn't mean we doesn't pay attention to the costs of each promotion or initiative; it just means that we haven't put an arbitrary 'ceiling' or 'floor' on how may dollars we'll spend that month, season, or year.

Instead, we focus on ROI: Return on Investment. We ask, in each case, "If we spend $3,000 on this event/promotion/mailing, how many dollars will that bring into the practice in the next month, quarter, year, lifetime?" And it's these two numbers – dollars in, dollars out – along with other important factors – that determine whether we'll spend that money.

Sure, there are instances when we simply have to say, "This is a great idea, but we can't afford it." But it's surprising how rarely that actually happens. Usually the really expensive stuff – TV ads, infomercials, massive traditional direct mail campaigns – get turned away *not* because of the "cash" issue, but because the ROI simply doesn't work, regardless of how big that buy-in number might be.

Remember, too, that it's not all dollars and sense. We are well aware that our practice has a role in the community, and that team members, from the doctors to the patient managers and back again, have personal preferences and goals. We take those *qualitative* factors into account alongside the *quantitative* factors, just as you do in looking at your household finances when you decide what non-profits you might be giving to or what churches or community organizations you'll be working with on a volunteer basis. An orthodontic practice, like any health-related business, has a role that goes beyond profit and loss, and we try our best not to forget that. It's a bit of a balancing act, but it's worth it. The end result keeps our team members paid *and* fulfilled, and both of those results are equally important.

In our practice, we look at the constant stream of requests for support as opportunities rather than headaches. In our case, our major non-profits, the ones we support the most, are Make-A-Wish and our local schools, but we always try to help out everybody, at least a little bit. It might be no more than thirty dollars for an ad in a yearbook or a community theater programs, but that does help get our name out there. But you have to ask yourself that same question every time: Is it worth it? Why? And if you can't make that case, as attractive as it may be and as much sympathy for the "cause" as you may feel …. you don't do it.

And do keep the "opportunity" aspect in mind. For instance, there are some times of year when we *know* the

Girl Scouts are coming. During certain seasons, we get at least ten Girl Scout troops a week stopping by the office, asking us to buy cookies. And as a general rule, we do: we try to buy one box from every girl who asks.

But then we *use* those cookies. We save them and give them to referring offices; we make it a 'special gift' we pass along. So not only are we sponsoring somebody, we're turning it around and making that pay off – a classic kind of ROI, that improves or reinforced our reputation along the way. And it's not just Girl Scouts. The Boy Scouts have taken to selling popcorn, and we buy that, too ... which goes out to our patients who have diabetes and can't have candy when they get their braces off. Once again: opportunity rather than obstacle.

Take your time and talk, talk, talk

So how do you achieve all these steps? Remember, first and foremost, that it's not a one-person show. If you give it some thought, you can probably come up with two or three other members of your team who are not only interested in helping to analyze the practice and set goals in the early stages of crunching numbers and sifting through reports but who have skills sets that can help. Recruit them. Buy them lunch. Give them some homework and set some specific deadlines and goals, so you don't find yourself sitting in your office at 11:30 p.m. on a Friday trying to do this all yourself. Your doctor or doctors may be part of this team or may not be – that's a personal preference – though obviously you'll keep them informed of the process every step along the way.

And speaking of keeping people informed: remember that internal goal of "total buy-in." That doesn't mean you put the entire staff on your goal-setting team but it *does* mean keeping them "in the loop" as you go.

I've found it helpful to talk about goals with the whole team at least three times in the process: first at the beginning, when you announce who the members of the "goal setting task force" are going to be … again about halfway through the process, when you share your thoughts about the kinds of goals and what matters most … and third, when you "pitch" the new or updated goals and ask for your team's acceptance and support. These three "phases" seem to avoid feelings of resentment and exclusion, and increase the chance that they'll get behind your final set of goals, even the 'stretch' goals and the ones that require commitment, because they feel they've been part of the process all along the way.

This doesn't have to be a full-day seminar or workshop for all involved. In fact, we put time-limits on each of these three meetings: half an hour for the first announcement, an hour (or less) for the check-in, and an hour (or less) for the final presentation. That way we don't eat up a lot of everyone's time, and they don't dread another awful, lengthy staff meeting.

And that "middle" meeting, the check-in, shouldn't be an empty, "Here's what we're doing, don't you worry" session. In fact, some member of your "core team" should be talking to every staff member about their own goals and their views of the practice goals – maybe in this meeting, maybe in private, depending on your own practice's culture and preferences. Ask them a few specific questions; take notes and bring it back to the core team. You may, in fact, find out that certain monetary or procedure goals that you think are very important really don't matter as much to others; you may realize that other metrics you're de-emphasized or missed are actually far better barometers of practice growth, health, and satisfaction.

Fifteen minutes to half an hour should be all your require, but there's real value in the "talk, talk, talk" portion of the goal-setting process, both in terms of setting sound and achieveable goals *and* in achieving that all-important buy-in.

Rinse and repeat

Finally – and this may go without saying – is to keep in mind that setting goals, measuring your progress, and modifying your goals and the plan is a *continuing process*. It would be great if it was a "one and done" affair, but the fact is you need to look at where you are on a regular basis, report your progress (or lack of process) to the whole team, and reward everyone who's involved in reaching those goals. In the practice I'm part of, we automatically add it to the agenda of team meetings every quarter, spend a little more time on it every six months, and then do the whole "Here's Where We Are" report once a year, as part of the presentation of the new year's goals.

If you start to look at goal-setting, goal-measurement, and goal-celebration as just a standard part of doing business, like paying the electricity bill and sending out payroll checks, it will rapidly come to feel less like a 'project' or a burden and more like a standardized step in running the practice properly. You'll even come to feel 'weird' if you don't do it on time.

After all, setting specific goals is a *good* thing, so when you reach them you can celebrate, and when you don't … you know why.

Chapter 4
Your Marketing Toolbox
Many possibilities, and how they can work for you

Now all the groundwork has been laid. You have come to understand your own practice and the patient population you serve, and you've set some goals that establish where you want the practice to go in the future.

But how to you get from *here* to *there*?

Here's one of the great things about practice marketing in the twenty-first century: you have a *huge* number of tools and opportunities that can help you reach your goals – tools you can use in face-to-face encounters and by using technology and social media.

And here's one of the not-so-great things about practice marketing in the twenty-first century: you have a huge number of tools and opportunities that can help you reach your goals! There are actually *too many* options, *too many* ways to go. It makes it almost impossible to know what to do first … or at all.

So how can you get started? How can you set priorities? And what do you not bother with at all?

Over the last few years, it's safe to say that my practice and the ones I consult with have tried virtually everything – twice. And we've been able to draw some conclusions, and establish some general rules about what works, what *might* work, and what's not worth the trouble.

Here are just a few of the many options available, in roughly alphabetical order:

Apps

Do you need a special phone app, just for your practice? Does anyone need it or use it? Truthfully: probably not. For a while, there was a big push from outside vendors to build special, "exclusive" apps just for our practice … but after much experimentation and measurement, and simply asking our patient base, we realized that having an app of our own wasn't worth the trouble. Having a fully outfitted and flexible web site and strong search engine optimization (see those sections below) seem to serve our patient base far better than *one more app* on their phone. Our patients tended to use it only a few times, if at all, or they delete it after a while, or simply forget it was there. And the cost of having an app created and the time it takes to get that done just didn't seem to be worthwhile. We haven't had one for months now, and it hasn't affected our practice growth in any significant way. In fact, it's freed up time for us to do more important things with social media and content marketing on our web site (see below again!). So think twice before you fall for those urgent-urgent sales pitches, like I did.

Billboards and Signage

All too often, investing in (and believing in) billboards, poster, graphics on the side of busses or at bus stops, and all the other endless variations of "signage" is more an act of faith than smart marketing. There's no way to measure the effectiveness of all that work; the only real value for outside ads like this is *name recognition* for your practice, and that often amounts to a small return on a big investment. You might be able to make a case for this medium in a highly competitive or highly urbanized market where there's an orthodontist on every corner and you need any edge you can get, or if you're a brand-new office where you need to establish your name in the market for the first time. That would make sense. But if you're an established practice just looking for growth, billboards are probably not a great investment.

Sure, it feels good for all concerned to see your practice name and doctor's head shots plastered on the side of public vehicles and hanging over major intersections. But ask yourself: do you *really* believe it brings in new customers, or keeps old ones coming back? If you can't say that with great confidence, consider investing that money elsewhere for a while and see if your new business traffic is affected in any way. You might be surprised.

Brochures
See "In-Office Brochures and Printed Pieces," below.

Business cards
Even in this day of dwindling paper products (see "Brochures" and "Print Advertising"), the good old-fashioned business card still has an important role to play.

Whether you (or your doctors and fellow team members) are attending an event, presenting a workshop, chatting at a barbecue or simply stuck in an elevator, a well-designed and high-quality business card can create a direct connection between your practice and a new patient or family.

And this isn't the place to cut costs. If you're going to invest in a business card – and you should – think of it more as a 'mini-brochure' than an old-fashioned one-sided single-color slab of paper (anybody can make those by the ream on their office printer these days). Have it professionally designed. Include your logo and consider a photograph of your doctor. Print on both sides, and be sure to include *all* the information about the practice:

- Practice Name
- Doctor Name (if it's different than the practice name)
- Street Address
- Phone number
- E-mail address for information
- Web site address
- Social media handles

Many practices go the extra step and have a *fold-over card* created; that affords you four panels to convey all the information a potential patient might want to know. For example, the four-panel card could also include:

- Your practice "log line" describing your specialty in a few choice words ("For your whole family," "Your Invisalign Specialist," "Same Day Service for Emergencies," etc.)

- "We accept all major insurance plans"
- A map
- Popular procedures or reputation-builders

… and four-panel, fold-over cards allow all your vital information to be larger and easier to read. It's worth considering

In any event, a business card is still an essential part of building your practice, even after all these years.

Community Outreach

You already know that your practice is an important part of the community … but take a moment to consider the full implications of that understanding. You have the power to help your community grow and grow stronger, and to expand your practice at the same time.

Choosing one or more local non-profit organizations to work with on a regular basis and making your practice a welcoming place for non-profits of all kinds is not only a great way to do the right thing as you build morale, it's a valid and vital part of practice growth, too.

If you haven't already chosen a worthwhile organization or school to work with, bring it up at your next all-team meeting. There are almost certainly schools or organizations that have a special connection for you, your doctors or other members of your team. Make a simple plan to reach out to those groups on an ongoing basis if you haven't already; participate in their fund-raisers, offer their informational brochures in your office, come up with some new educational and fund-raising partnerships that are fun and easy to publicize through both organizations.

At the same time, consider doing some community-building of your own. In our practice, we have had tremendous success with a scholarship program aimed at high school seniors. We make it work this way: Every year we offer a $1,000 college scholarship to the best essay that's submitted by our younger patients, past and present, on the subject of "Embrace Your Smile." There are no other parameters; we know that topic means something different to everyone. But we publicize it widely, through e-mails, announcements on our web site, posts on social media, and in flyers in the office, as well as at all the schools we work with (see "Events: School Visits, below). After the deadline, each of our doctors gets to pick one essay they like the most. Since we have three doctors, those three 'finalists' are then read by everyone on staff, and we take a vote. Then we invite the winner to the office, where we present a check, take some pictures and proudly announce the results everywhere we can (and usually the student's school is more than happy to spread the word as well). We even make it a surprise and do the "big check" thing, so the pictures are terrific. We've even had them picked up by local newspapers.

The fact is, this is one of the biggest events we have every year. It gets more "likes" on our Facebook page than almost anything else. It's a genuine "feel-good" moment that works for everyone.

And of course it doesn't stop with a single organization or a single scholarship. There are plenty of groups in town that deserve your attention: Girl Scouts, Boy Scouts, Little League, Pee Wee Football, high school sports teams … the list is virtually endless. In many cases, these groups will only want a little – your participation in a single event or a few boxes of cookies. If they know that your practice is a welcoming place that's always willing to pitch in, you'll find it not only helps your community, but it makes your practice more popular and all the members of your team proud to work there.

It's the definition of "win/win."

Discount cards

Along with the all-important business card and practice brochure (see those sections for more details), we've found one other piece of printed material that has served us well, over and over: the discount card.

This is a simple, easy-to-produce product, standard business-card size. It features:

- Your practice name and logo
- The words "DISCOUNT CARD," nice and big
- The discount you're offering, in equally big letters
- The practice address and phone number
- Any restrictions on the offer (e.g., "may be combined with insurance but no other offer," and/or "New Patients Only," etc.

In our practice, we have chosen two separate offers: *Complimentary Consultation and X-Rays* and *$250 Off your first procedure.* The card that we've created has the words **$250 OFF!** in BIG letters, and the whole card is printed in bright colors, looking more like a coupon than a business card. It is coated – "shiny" – only on one side, so whoever is handing out the card can easily write on the back, adding the event or a name to personalize it. There is no expiration date on the offer, though we change the color scheme every time we reprint (which seems to be about every six months), so we can roughly gauge how old the cards are when they come in. We're constantly surprised when cards from a year ago or more show up, but it's a regular occurrence.

It has been a huge success. We give our discount cards away freely, with and without our practice brochures, at community events, school visits, to referring practices and at presentations of all kinds. We are genuinely delighted when they are used, and we make sure that the new patient knows that – no sour looks or sighs when they hand the card to us. In fact, the Discount Card is our second most successful strategy for getting new patients in the door, right behind practice referrals – inexpensive, easy, and effective.

E-mailing for new patients

There was a time – a *short* time – when e-mail replaced traditional mail as a valid and powerful practice-building tool. Sadly, those days are over.

Maybe e-mail was just too easy. After a very short

honeymoon, everyone started sending everyone else far too much unwanted promotional material, and soon no one was opening any of it. Today, we don't use e-mail marketing to attract new patients at all, not even "new resident" campaigns. We have found the mailing lists that can be purchased are not only very expensive but often inaccurate or incomplete, and the rate at which those e-mail are opened or responded to is so low it's virtually non-existent. Though we are 'pitched' the use of e-mail campaigns by outside services on a regular basis, we learned the lesson the hard way: it's not a solid strategy for practice growth.

E-mailing your existing patients

E-mail is still a valuable tool in staying in touch with your current patient base and keeping them involved ... but be careful and selective in its use. Remember, even your most loyal patients get *way* too much e-mail every day, so they frequently assume that something unsolicited, even from an old friend like you, is "junk mail."

Don't ignore e-mail to your patient base, but when you use it, make sure you are *saying something important* to them or *making an offer that benefits them greatly*. Yes, we still do the occasional "e-mail blast" when we have a great promotion, and it does increase the number of office visits, but it's not a constant barrage. And for every promotion we send, we also send holiday greetings and congratulations (like the winners of our scholarships – see "Community Outreach" for more on that) that have nothing to do with 'selling.' Over time, we've built up a reputation with our patient base that an e-mail from our practice is about *something that matters to them*, and we've seen our "open" rates slowly increase. But we know that a few too many promo's or blasts of empty PR fluff can undo all that good work very quickly.

Something more: many practices still spend a lot of time and effort doing e-mailed newsletters to the patient base. We did the same for quite a while, but when we had a change in staff and a very busy month we missed one … and then two … and then realized that no patients had asked about it, our return-visit rate was the same, and all the important communications we had with patients were continuing without a hitch, easily handled by phone calls and web site. So we never went back.

We have also stopped using e-mail to send out appointment reminders. It was a key part of appointment management for quite a while, but when we started asking patients if they would prefer getting a phone call, a text, or an e-mail, the overwhelming response was 'text' or 'call' … and almost no one even put e-mail on the list.

One final bit of advice: when you *do* use e-mails to talk to a patient, avoid attachments. Many spam filters will flag any e-mail with an attachment these days, even from known correspondents, and many patients simply won't open them for fear of malware or phishing. Embed the important parts of what you have to say in the e-mail itself, and/or refer them to your web site for more information. You'll get a much higher, more appreciative response.

Events

Technology is great. Promoting the practice so much easier and more flexible because of it. But as it turns out, face-to-face contact, through referrals, in-office conversations and events, still remain the most important, productive, and engaging ways to acquire new patients and keep established patient families coming back.

Every month – every week, in fact – we create or participate in events that keep our practice top-of-mind and draw people into the office. We use our practice brochures, business cards and discount cards all the time, everywhere we go. We have established "elevator pitches" so we can describe the practice, its unique specialties, and its advantages to patients in a few well-chosen, often-repeated words. The result is a steady stream of new and returning patients that form the backbone of our practice growth plan.

Here are just a few of the kinds of events we create or are a part of:

- **Community Events.** We've discussed this elsewhere in this book (see Chapter 3), but it's worth mentioning again: community festivals, summer camps, art walks, health days, music and performance get-togethers ... wherever members of the community gather for fun or education, we're there. We have a booth and materials; we have members of the team who genuinely love the contact; we have standard give-aways and prizes we can offer at a moment's notice, and we use our phones to take as many pictures as we possibly can that we feature on our social media all the time (see "Social Media," elsewhere in this chapter).

Community events like these have become a major factor in growing the practice and establishing our reputation in town – so much so that many other orthodontic practices, as well as pediatricians, primary care providers, chiropractors and other healthcare professionals now show up at the same events and do the same thing. So here are just a few hints on how to make community events marketing effective and, believe it or not, easy and fun:

- Establish a "kit" that includes materials, signage, even table cloths, pens, crayons and banners that can be 'broken out,' repacked, and replenished easily. There's no need to re-invent the wheel every time you venture out.
- Build an Events Calendar that "rolls forward" for the next twelve months, so you know what events are coming, what your commitments already are, and who's going to take the lead. Post that calendar in a prominent place – the break room, maybe? – so everyone knows what's coming up next.
- Create and refine the 'elevator message' – the simple, sixty-seconds-or-less "speech" that team members can use

to describe the practice, its unique benefits, and its most popular services quickly and clearly. Make sure that everyone who works at the events knows the message and has been trained to memorize it and use it smoothly.

- Design a simple form to capture names and e-mail addresses, and have a "fish bowl" always available for potential patients to drop in their business cards or notes. Capturing e-mail addresses from interested community members whenever you can, and knowing what to do with those, is key!

- Identify the members of the office staff who truly enjoy this kind of public contact. Train them in using the "elevator message," and schedule them for specific events ... but don't overuse any one person. Avoid burn-out. And think creatively about what you can do to compensate your 'star players' for their help – cash bonuses, extra days off, gift cards, etc. Their time and energy is important and valuable, and they shouldn't be taken advantage of or seen as "volunteers" or "just doing their job."

- Have a standard e-mail and a simple procedure for follow-up: an easily customizable message that goes out right after the events – within 48 hours if possible – to all the potential patient names you gathered, telling them how much you enjoyed meeting them, thanking them for their interest, and re-offering the "Discount Card" deal – the free consultation or dollars off. Be sure to include a link to your web site so they can sign up for their first appointment, and refer them to your social media where they can see pictures of the event (and maybe themselves). And finally, be sure that the e-mail comes from a specific person on your team (even if they didn't actually send it themselves), rather than from the practice overall or no one in particular. The less it looks like a form letter and the more it looks like a personal communication, the better.

Our involvement in community events, large and small (well, medium-sized) has become a standard, weekly part of our practice activity, and a significant factor in our growth. It can be the same for you.

- **Field Trips to your office** are hugely important as well. Combined with the school trips (see below), we have found that inviting classes into the office, where the kids can meet the doctors and other team members, see and touch some of the exotic technology and walk away with "door prizes" and dental hygiene kits of their own can make a huge impression – on the kids, the teachers, and even on the parents who weren't there. This is especially important for children who are being home-schooled, or for small private schools where an on-site visit can't be worked out. We reach out to home-schoolers through web sites, Facebook groups, and other social media to set up specific office visits just for them, and the results have been highly productive.

- **School Events** are among the most important and productive tactics we use to bring in new families. These tend to be very "seasonal;" we focus on two times of the year for most of them: February for Dental Health Month and October for Orthodontic Health Month.

  School visits have been part of our practice growth for a long time, so we have built up a strong "contact list" and equally strong relationships with the schools in our area. They are very happy to work with us, because we've developed presentations that aren't just 'sales pitches" for the practice.

They are educational programs that they value, on how to take care of their teeth, on sports and safety issues, on healthy diets and drinks. We have games that we play and a couple of different videos that help with the educational component. (**Toothfairy Island** offers some great curriculum that we are happy to use. You can take a look at what they have to offer at www.toothfairyisland.com.)

We also make sure that the presentations we offer are *age appropriate.* Nothing turns a kid off quicker than being talked down to. So we have dental education materials for very small kids, like puzzles of the teeth, lips, and tongue; we have more advanced materials for tweens and teens about diet and self-care – a different lesson for every age group.

"Refresh" the content every year, too. The kids remember, and though there may be favorite games or give-aways, they've come to expect something new (but equally fun!) each time they see you. You don't want to go in and preach the same lesson every year to every kid; quite the opposite, you want them to looking forward to you coming in.

(I learned this the hard way when I made a visit to a K-3 school in our area with the same program I'd taken a year ago, and was greeted with a chorus of "We've already seen this!" and a room full of bored and restless kids. Never again!)

All this means, of course, that you have to plan in advance – *far* in advance, in some cases. I set aside time in the summer to set up the program for October, and budget time in the fall for the February events.

And pay special attention to the "treats" that you leave behind. Some are perennial favorites, but you want to keep switching it up. And parcel out those treats as you go: pass out prizes for asking questions. give them pencils to write down a time for tooth-brushing, distribute water bottles when you talk about hydration. And of course, everybody gets a bag at the end of the presentation: a new toothbrush and paste, floss, and – of course! -
- a discount card for them to pass along to their parents. (The discount card works as a 'tracking device,' too, so you can gauge just how important and productive the event really is.)

I can't emphasize how valuable school visits have become for us. Today, these visits are one of our four largest sources for new business. We work with over 17 schools, and present to more than 3,400 children. I know that for sure, because that's how many treat-bags we distributed last year. So even if school visits are something you already do, take a look at them and see how that program might be expanded or improved. You'll almost certainly see positive gains for your effort.

- **Holiday Events** are great morale-builders for your staff, fodder for your social media, and community builders that actually result in new patient growth as well. And we're not just talking about the obvious "paid holiday" list of Thanksgiving, Christmas, and the Fourth of July. Check the many available on-line calendars of the slightly crazier holidays that are out there (One of our favorites, for instance, in National Hot Chocolate Day!). You can't celebrate every single one, but you *can* do something, big or small, every couple of weeks.

This is an opportunity to get your staff involved as well. Have them decide on some of the events themselves; let them create something new and fun. Your patients – whether they're coming in for a scheduled visit or just cruising their Instagram or Facebook timeline – love to see that you're enjoying yourself and engaging your families. Mardi Gras, St. Patrick's Day, obviously Halloween – we do them all, and we take videos and pictures with our phone all the time.

Can the value of holiday promotions be measured as completely and accurately as school visits or field trips? Not really. But their importance to team morale and community relations can't be argued or ignored.

In-office brochures

The practice brochure is a central and essential tool for marketing. Like the business cards and discount cards, it's something that needs plenty of attention and regular updates.

Your practice brochure is so important, in fact, that I have only one very serious bit of advice to give you about it: *hire a professional.* Much of what you and your practice works on every day – the face-to-face communications, the in-office relationships and patient relations, even the social media – are "home-grown" efforts and should be. But the practice brochure that will do you the most good should be created by people who make effective and beautiful marketing materials for a living. We personally work with Practice Marketer (at **www.PracticeMarketer.com**), and there are other reputable ones as well, and you'll find a short section at the end of this chapter that gives some advice on choosing the best vendors for this kind of work.

Still, there are a few guidelines for your practice brochure that you'll want to make double-sure are there:

- Photographs are better than drawings or diagrams; they help create a personal connection between the potential patients and the doctor/practice
- Stock photos can be good, but having 'real' pictures of your actual doctor(s) and team members is very effective and often worth the effort

- When it comes to words, less is more. The brochure should be easy to read, generous with white space, and use bullet points and headlines. It should convey the message about the practice's specialties and greatest benefits *at a glance*, and often images and headlines do that better than lots of long, gray paragraphs

- The brochure, like any piece that markets your practice, should feature a prominent *call to action* – a phone number or web site (or both!), and clear instructions on what you want the reader to do next: call for an appointment, log on for more information, *come in*. You can never go wrong by being direct and simple, and telling potential patients *exactly* what you want them to do next

Finally: as important as the practice brochure may be, it's not a 'one-time' thing. You should revisit the brochure at least once a year, or after any major change in the practice, and do your best to look at it with fresh eyes. Is it still accurate? Does it reflect what the practice is doing and can do? Have the desires or needs of your patient base evolved since the last time you looked carefully at the brochure? In this day and age, revisions to a good design are relatively easy and inexpensive, and for something as important as this brochure, being accurate, attractive, and effective is important … today and tomorrow.

Internet advertising

These days, search engines and social media like Google

AdWords, Facebook, Twitter and the rest are working very hard to make money, and that often means trying to sell you advertising. They give you discounts on ad plans, free credits for ads, and what sounds like very good reasons to invest in them.

My personal experience – in my own practice and with many others I've spoken with and worked with – is that advertising like this, for an individual or even group practice, rarely pays off. That's not to say you shouldn't experiment with online advertising (see "Test, Test, and Test Again," below), but for me it is very much a "prove it" proposition. As much as we would all like it to be otherwise, the most consistently successful tactics for practice growth are the old standards – referrals, events, and search engine optimization – and these are *gradual*; they build up over time. There aren't any quick fixes, fast strategies, or simple switches to flip. And all too often, internet advertising is presented as one of these, rather than as part of a larger, more careful marketing plan.

Postcards and other mailers

Much like print advertising (see below), postcards and direct mail were a mainstay of practice marketing for decades, and every practice in America still gets a steady stream of pitches, presentations, and pleas from advertising agencies – local and virtual – to convince them of the value of frequent and expensive direct mail. Also like print advertising … its day has passed.

A single, professionally produced practice brochure is still an important tool for you to have (see "In-office Brochures" for more on this), and of course business cards are still essential (see "Business Cards" for details). But beyond that, postcards or other printed pieces specifically designed to be mailed are a thing of the past, and probably not worth the expense.

This has to do with the fundamental change in the way that people choose their health care, including dentistry and orthodontia. In the past, when they need to make that choice – when they move into the neighborhood, when their kids become old enough to need an orthodontist, when their current caregivers retire or close up shop – individuals *used* to go to the Yellow Pages or the local newspaper to see what their options were. Not today. Today they ask their friends – as always – and they go to Google or another search engine (*are* there other search engines?) for the most likely results, then dig a little deeper by looking at Yelp! other review sites, and the web sites of the individual practices. They look for the best-known, most respected, and most prominent practices in town that clearly match their needs and expectations. And ultimately that's what all the marketing, community relations, and advertising is about: to be that practice.

Unfortunately, direct mail doesn't seem to find those people at the right time, or communicate to them in a way that works. Look to the other tried-and-true tactics instead.

Print advertising

If you're more than thirty years old, you remember very clearly when *print advertising* was the backbone of practice growth. Ads in the local daily and weekly newspapers, an expensive but high-profile ad in the city magazine or the Sunday supplement, display ads in parents' magazines, children's magazines, regional magazines. And most important of all, Yellow Pages ads. You simply couldn't hope to survive without the Yellow Pages.

Then along came the internet ... and everything changed. Within a very few years, the number of daily newspapers dropped catastrophically. Today you're lucky if there's even one daily newspaper in your area. The number and page-count of free weekly publications has plunged as well; potential patients simply don't read or refer to them in the numbers they used to – not anymore. And today the very existence of "telephone books" (remember them?) is in jeopardy.

Because of all these changes, I can tell you my practice doesn't invest any significant money in print advertising. We may spend a few dollars to make an appearance in a program for a big local event or theatrical production, but that's more of an investment in public relations than "sales." We support our community and non-profits that matter to us in this way, with no expectations about bringing in new patients.

The one possible exception *might* be experimenting with print ads in a popular free-distribution weekly in your area – but only *experimenting* with it, not *committing* to it, and only when you have a specific event or promotion (an appearance at a local festival, a big lecture or presentation in town) coming up … and even then, only in conjunction with your normal promotional plan, using your web site, social media, and patient e-mails.

If you do decide to give traditional display advertising a try, be sure to measure the response by including a coupon or promotional code in the ad (for a free gift or a free chance in a drawing), so you can measure its effectiveness. Depending on the event and the publication, there *may* be some value in this kind of highly focused, infrequent advertising … but be sure there's a good return on that investment before you move forward.

Other than that … look to the internet. Like it or not, it's where the action is this century.

Search Engine Optimization and Patient Review Sites

Along with events and referrals, your presence in search engines – primarily Google – and your powerful, positive reputation as consistently shown in review sites like Yelp! are key to your practice growth. But let's be honest: understanding the constantly changing landscape of SEO and Yelp! algorithms is a full-time job, that – like the work of your orthodontists – is best left to the professionals.

Save yourself some heartache and many wasted hours by aligning yourself with an SEO consultant you can trust

– someone who will make sure you appear at the top of any reasonable search parameters, and who can make sure that the ratings and reviews that potential patients will find are positive and up-to-date.

Beth Leach of Practice Marketer (www.PracticeMarkter.com) was kind enough to sit down for an interview with me to talk about SEO and reputation management. You'll find that as the next chapter in this book. Read it, and then find yourself the powerful allies you deserve. You'll need them … and your practice will thrive because of them.

Social Media

Like it or not, social media is the centerpiece of your practice's presence on the web. It's difficult to measure their importance, but there's no doubt that the people who make decisions about which orthodontist to use and when to use them are deeply influenced by the social media the decision-makers use. In the case of orthodontic services, there have been plenty of studies telling us that *women*, especially *mothers*, are the primary decision-makers, not only for themselves but for all the members of their family including their spouses, and at this point in time – 2018 – Facebook continues to be the social media platform of choice for this particular subgroup.

Of course, this doesn't mean that other platforms, both established and emerging, can be ignored. Twitter seems to be a mainstay, though generally it is less well-used by young mothers; InstaGram seems to be on the rise, and not just among young people (though they seem to favor it). Pinterest is still a factor; so is YouTube. Even LinkedIn has its place with professionals, and the only thing we know for certain is that there will be another platform – one none of us have ever heard of – coming into view sooner rather than later.

The important thing to remember is that *they can't be ignored*. Someone in our office posts to Facebook every day. The pictures from our in-office events or community events go up on our own web site (see below); we use the practice accounts on all the media to announce promotions, appearances, in-office events, giveaways and other activities.

How do we choose which ones to use? We regularly ask our patients, both old and new, "What's your favorite app? Found anything new?" We talk about it at team meetings on a regular basis, and we occasionally experiment with promotions that appear only on a single platform like Pinterest or LinkedIn to gauge whether they seem to be growing in importance or losing their luster. Things tend to change slowly, but they *do* change, and we keep an eye on the tidal effects all the time.

Who does all the work? The answer tends to be "everybody." Certain people in the office seem to enjoy social media more than others; almost everyone has a single platform – Facebook or Twitter or InstaGram are the current favorites – that they enjoy the most. We tend to parcel out the work to those who enjoy it the most, as in "Why don't you get the pictures from the holiday party up on Facebook?" If it's someone who enjoys doing it and knows the platform well, it takes only a couple of minutes and it's done with genuine enthusiasm – and that shows.

Generally speaking, we don't do as much "interactivity" with social media as is often recommended. There's nothing wrong with surveys or open-ended questions that lead to dialogue, but managing the responses (and often unintended consequences) can take a lot of time and lead nowhere. By and large, we use social media on a daily basis as a combination of newsletter and billboard, to let current and hopefully future patients and their families look into the practice and what we're doing, rather than use it as a back-and-forth tool of communication. In that regard, social media have worked well for us without become a detrimental "time-suck."

You might want to start asking your patients what their favorite platform is and discussing the results in your next team meeting. There might be some fresh information there.

Your web site

Your web site is a key part of practice management and growth, but it's not exactly like the other parts of the machine. It is, at least in part, the *destination* that all of your events, promotions, referral efforts, and advertising lead to: your exclusive place on the internet that answers all the questions about your practice that patients may have, allows new and returning patients to make appointments, offers updates on what's happening, provide information to new and potential referrers and the media, and ideally becomes a resource about orthodontics and dental health in general.

Like logo design, the brochure, SEO and reputation development, web site design is one of the area where you need to bring in a carefully chosen and trusted professional. All the major hosting companies and web developers like SquareSpace and WordPress and Wix, among so many others, like to tell you how easy it is for you to "do it yourself," but when it comes to your practice's site, you're far better off working with a respected and experienced pro.

How do you find the right ally? Ask around. Take some time to browse the internet and find other orthodontic web sites in other areas that you think look and 'feel' good – that do the things you want them to do. Take a few notes, check the footers of those web sites, and maybe even send those practices an e-mail to ask who they worked with to develop the site. You'll hear certain names coming up more than once.

As you make your choice, take these factors into consideration:

- You want someone who's experienced in orthodontic practice marketing, not just making web site in general or even just marketing in general.
- You want someone who's easy to talk to, doesn't indulge in jargon or vague generalities. Specifics are good.
- The cost and timetable should be clear from the outset: how long will it take and what's the budget? If you can't get a straight answer to

either question, or there are "escape clauses" that could change the delivery date or add costs in unexpected ways ... keep looking.

- Take your time and find the right person or company to work with. You will almost certainly be coming back to them for updates and improvements; ideally, you're looking for a long-term relationship.

Just as important: even when you find the right web developer, you need to stay involved every step of the way. This isn't a matter of just dumping the assignment on someone, new or well-known, and saying, "make it pretty." You should walk into the selection and design process with a pretty strong idea of what you want the site to look like and "feel" like and what you want it to do.

What a patient (or you) can do on the site is referred to as "functionalities," and it's worth the time to build a list of those before you begin. Here are just a few of the most common traits and functionalities that an orthodontic web site should have:

- The look should be clean and very professional. Images that appear in your practice brochure can and should appear here as well; the same logo, type fonts, and images should appear on line and on paper.
- The site should be easy to use and understand at a glance. First-time visitors should have no trouble understanding and navigating the site,

even if it does and says a lot of different things. It doesn't need to be crowded or over-active, with animations and special effects. It needs to be friendly and easy-to-use.

- As with the practice brochure, photographs are better than diagrams or line art, and fewer words are better than too many.
- Better to have a lot of pages that do one thing well than a single page that tries to be all things to all people. If you can't figure out what a page is there for and how it works within just a few seconds, it's either poorly designed or too complicated. (And a good web designer will know that.)
- Patients should be able to schedule appointments, ask questions, and get directions to your office with no more than a click or two of the mouse.
- There should be a separate page for recent events, promotions, and practice news.
- There should be a page of testimonials that patients can add to themselves (and that someone in your office updates and 'cleans up' on a regular basis, to keep the best and most recent testimonials at the top and stop mischief-makers before they get started.)
- There should be a page for referring practices as well, both current and potential, that helps to build and maintain relationships with this important source for new business.
- If you decide to have a blog or a Q&A section

about dental health, the practice, new technology or all of the above, make sure that the design of the web site makes it easy for team members to add new content and photographs without being programmers or designers themselves. The developer should be willing to train, or at last supply "how to" instructions, to anyone on staff who wants to be involved in those updates, and they shouldn't need hours of special education or experience to be part of the process.

- There should be a prominent place on the front page that asks, "What do you think of this web site?" and where visitors can leave questions that will be promptly answered by a team member. You can gain valuable insights and often head off potential headaches by having an "open portal" on the front page, where it's easy to find.

- It should be easy for you and other key members of your team to look at and understand site statistics: how many visitors the site has had, what they're looking at and how long they stay, even what time of the day or week there is the most activity. It may not be important on a day-to-day basis, but as you make regular reviews of the site, this information can be of great value to you and your developers, and point you in the right direction for further improvement and refinement.

Your web site is your "face" on the internet. It is seen by more people than you, your doctor, and all your patients combined, so it deserves close attention and regular improvement. You don't need to be an expert at web marketing or design yourself, but you need to have a couple of people like that on your team, and you need to be an active participant in your 'presence on the web" as time goes on.

A special word about Referrals

There are two kinds of referrals that bring your practice more new patients than any other single source: *referrals from patients* and *referrals from other practices*. Let's talk a little about them both.

Referrals from patients

We talked a bit about in-office conversations and patient referrals back in Chapter Two. Take a moment to go back and read that again.

The message is clear: your best allies for practice growth are satisfied and enthusiastic patients. After all, virtually all kinds of advertising and marketing are trying to duplicate or enhance the most important act in practice building: a friend giving valuable advice to a friend, telling them, "You should go here." That's called "word of mouth," and it's ultimately what all this is about.

You're already doing the single most successful thing to build word of mouth: providing excellent care to your patients. The second, almost as essential, aspect of enhancing word of mouth is to *ask them to spread the word.* You can do that in person and in correspondences, though social media and in e-mails. You can incentivize it with gifts and giveaways. But most important, you *can't* assume that even your most enthusiastic patients will tell others about your practice *unless you ask them to.* So make it a habit: ask for referrals and encourage them to spread the word.

And the first essential factor in building referrals: *say thank you.* Those may be the two most powerful words in the English language.

When you get a referral, send a quick note saying *thank you for sending Sarah our way.* Include a gift card from Starbucks or Amazon or Best Buy. Make a note in their patient file so you can thank them in person the next time they come into the office for an appointment. And yes, gifts are nice and very effective but the simple acknowledgement, that *thank you*, is the most important piece of all.

Referrals from dentists and other practices

I could write a whole book on referral marketing (and maybe I will!), but for the moment, keep these three things in mind:

- Referrals from other practices are your single most important source for new business

- Keep track of who your best referrals are, down to the smallest useful detail
- Thank them and incentivize them regularly. *Very* regularly

We treat our referring practices like the gold they are. We have a "points" system that allows us to assess who our most active referrers are; we have a rotating and ever-growing list of incentives for our top referrers; we even have a special page on our web site just for them, where they can let us know when they've seen a patient we share. And we make a point of sending patients we share *back* to the referring dental offices for cleanings or other services, and then give them credit for serving their patients. Everyone wins, and it brings us even closer (and more permanently) together.

I also make a point of knowing everything I can about the whole *team* of people who work for our referrers. Birthdays, anniversaries, the birthdays of children, even practice birthdays. I review that information before each visit, and update it after I leave their offices. That way I can call everyone by name, remember their children's names and basketball games, and what gifts they liked most (and didn't like). Being aware of that particular office's preferences goes a long way.

The variety of gifts and incentives continues to grow. Once a month, we give away CE credits, we have a referring practice 'lunch and munch," and we always keep that door open for something more. I also use PraticeGenius.com to stage contests and handle rewards fulfillment.

I make a point of visiting every referring practice in our area at least once a month – the top referrers even more often. I never forget that referring practices are our bread and butter, and I make sure that *they* know I value them as well. It's an investment of time and energy that's paid off over and over.

Final Word Number One: Test, test, and test some more

There is so much to do, so many possibilities; that it's hard to know where to start. And it's just as hard to know *when to stop*, especially when you realize ... you can't.

Yes, there are some tried-and-true 'centers' that you can never ignore – referrals and events, as we've discussed above. But modern practice marketing is also so involved in new technologies and social media that you can never rest on your laurels. There's always something new to try.

In future chapters, we'll talk about planning your marketing efforts ... and part of that plan, as difficult as it may be at times, is to *plan to test*. What may not work for most practices (things like e-newsletters or Google AdWords) may, in fact, be perfect for your particular practice or patient population. So try those. Don't spend a lot of money or a huge amount of time, and don't take *anybody's* word for "what's best." As you can see, there are remarkably few generalities in practice marketing. We are all roughly the same and all very different, so try your best to set aside some time in your team meetings and in your month to test new ideas – even slightly crazy ones! – and build a marketing plan that's unique to you and your goals.

It's easier said than done, I know…but it's so worth it!

Final Word Number Two: The Power of the Doctor

It's your impulse – and partly your job – to do things *for* your doctor or doctors. That's why you're there: so they don't have to do it all themselves. However …

The practice is built around your doctor or doctors, and they have tremendous power. That's worth remembering, and using when it matters. Doctor involvement – in photographs, at events, for presentations – has a huge and positive effect on present and future patients, so whenever it's possible to involve them, try and make that happen.

It can be as little as a ten-minute talk in the middle of an hour-long visit, or a single photograph that includes them in the team. Quotes in an article, blogs under their by-line – almost any "doctor involvement" or a regular basis will pay off in the long run. At its very best, your practice is a *person-to-person* endeavor, and the doctor is the "person" at one end of that equation. Whenever your doctor's involved, whenever they jump in … the patients, new and long-established, notice that, and it's huge.

So who's supposed to do all this?

That answer comes in two parts:

(1) Everyone in the office …

(2) …guided by one special person

Make no mistake: practice marketing on this scale is not a part-time job. You have to be constantly on top of things, you have to be available on weekends and evenings, and sometimes the hours are long. You have to be *committed*, and you have to actually enjoy this kind of work.

It can be great fun, but don't forget it's competitive as well. The patient population and the media landscape are constantly changing, and if you're not out front, someone else is going to step ahead of you,

If you're the one doing the work, you need to ask yourself if you're the right person to be at the center of this storm. If you're the one looking for someone *else* to be that person, make sure that your candidate truly, sincerely, loves this kind of work. You can't force someone to attend these events, visit these other practices, talk to these patients if they don't really want to be there. If you try, you'll never reach your goals.

As you look for the right person – or as you look at yourself – ask if this is, in fact, the face you want representing the practice … and will they love doing it?

If they – or you – are like me, then the answer to both those questions is "yes." And for people like that – like *us* – the adventure is just beginning.

Chapter 5
Search Engines, Optimization, Reviews and Reputation
An interview with Beth Leach of PracticeMarketer.com

How do potential patients find your practice? Referrals are very important; community involvement is essential. But the reality is that the internet, search engines like Google (frankly, mostly Google alone), and reviews sites like Yelp! are just as important as any other promotional effort you make. In fact, in some communities and for some practices, SEO and reviews are *the* most important thing.

Working with the internet is not for the faint-hearted. It takes training, experience, and a lot of time. That's why this is an area that – as I've said elsewhere in this book – I look to professionals for help.

I was lucky enough to find and start working with Beth Leach years ago. She is the founder of PracticeMarkter.com and PraticeRetriever.com, and she's been working in this field for many years. And she's been instrumental in the growth of the practices I work with; I recommend her all the time.

So when I came to this part of the book – the part about search engines, search engine optimization (a mouthful that is always referred to as "SEO"), and how to generate and manage online reviews, I decided to go straight to the expert. I sat down with Beth for a series of talks about how potential patients use the internet in all its many forms to find local practices, choose which one to go to, and review that practice before making a final choice.

Here's what she had to say ...

Google and Search Engine Optimization (SEO)

Thanks for talking with me, Beth. Let me start by asking a really basic question: how important is Google and Yelp!, along with other search engines and review sites, to growing an orthodontic practice?

Beth: I don't think it's possible to over-estimate how important Google, Yelp!, and your own web site really are. We all know how important personal referrals are; they're a cornerstone of every practice growth plan. But like it or not, potential patients use the internet – their phones, their tablets, their personal computers – to get their own referrals these days, and that's a trend that will only expand in the future. If you want to execute a successful practice growth plan, you *have* to include building and maintaining a good online presence, and that includes a web site, lots of good reviews, and search engine optimization.

What exactly is "Search Engine Optimization"?

Beth: It's a fancy term for a very simple result – one that you and probably everyone you know goes through every day. You're looking for an answer to a question. You use your phone, tablet, or computer to log onto Google, and you type in your question, in plain English or just as key words, and Google presents you with a list of links to web sites or online resources that best answer to the question you ask.

But how does Google decide which web sites, which resources to show, and in what order? They do it using a complicated and constantly changing set of *algorithms*, basically mathematical formulas, to decide which are the 'best answers for the questioners.

When it comes to orthodontic practices, the question that is almost always asked of Google and other search engines is something like, "Orthodontists in Anytown, Minnesota." And when that question is typed in to Google, you want *your* practice to be one of the very first ones that shows up – really, the *first* one – with a listing that shows you in your very best light. The process of making sure you're at the "top of the charts" in any search engine query is called "Search Engine Optimization," and that's one of the things that my company specializes in.

So what is Google looking for? What puts you at the top of the results?

Beth: The answer to that is constantly changing. Very basically, Google's algorithm is always looking for practices with a *good online presence* ... but what does that mean? How do they determine that?

It changes all the time. Every month or two, Google comes out with updates to their algorithms, and the algorithm determines where your practice is going to be placed on line. Generally, this means that every couple of months the whole SEO world goes around and tries to figure out what that algorithm is, how it's changed, and how they can use it better.

Your goal is pretty simple. When the potential patient types in "Orthodontist in Anytown," or "Invisalign in Anytown," you want your name to come up first. Not in the 'ad's portion off to one side, but in what's called the 'organic' part of Google, the part that's underneath the ads, underneath the maps (if they happen to have Maps on that page). That's where you want to be. Anybody can put in ads all around you, but the organic results are what people are really interested in, and where you'll see the highest likelihood of finding people who will become patients. Also: those maps listings are very important, too. They are also called "Local Listings," and they are a huge part of how you're found online.

Generally speaking, if a potential patient asks for

"Orthodontists in Anytown," they'll be given a "three-pack" by Google: three practices in the area that match the requirements that Google is looking for. That doesn't mean these are the only three practices in the area – not at all. That's what the algorithm decides. And updates to the algorithm can change those results from one day to the next. For instance, a while ago Google did the "Possum Update," that changed everything for dental practices. After Possum, if your practice was less than one minute's walking distance from *another* orthodontic practice in the neighborhood, the Google algorithm decides which practice had the best SEO at that moment, and *only* showed that one. The other practice might be taken off the map completely or ranked much lower. In some cases that second practice would still have a Google Maps listing, but didn't show up under that keyword. And it's very difficult to fight this decision; you have to look at a lot of things to get back up there.

So why does a practice get kicked out of that 'three-pack' to begin with?

Beth: It's generally not just one thing; it's a combination of factors. But here are the first and most important ones we always look at:

- **Name, Address, and Phone Number (NAP).** It seems obvious, but it's very important: *everywhere your practice is listed, it should have exactly the same name, address and phone number.* This is usually referred to as the "NAP." You'd think this would be easy. You've probably had the practice name for a long time, and your address and phone number haven't changed. *But ...* if you bought your practice in the last twenty years, the previous owner's name still might be popping up now and then. If you've changed the name of your practice in the last twenty years, even a little bit, you might have this same issue. For instance, you may call yourself "John Smith Orthodontics" today, but ten years ago, back in the days of Yellow Pages and newspaper ads, you called yourself "John Smith, DMD, MS." For one thing, you should know that name change has to be re-registered with the state as a different fictitious name, and it also has to be put into Google all over again, presented properly with all the documents to all the different search engines. Not just Google; Google pulls form a hundred different places. If you've moved your office in the last twenty years, that can cause problems, too. If you have a suite number that's changed, even something as small as listing it as "Suite A" back in 2004 and now it's "Number A," that causes a problem. There are a hundred things that can cause an NAP issue. Fortunately, NAP is an easy thing to fix, but it has to be done and re-checked regularly.

- **Number Two: multiple listings of your practice in Google and other search engines.** You may not know it, but many practices have this, simply because they're been around a long time and a lot of people have done a lot of things on the internet over the years. There may be one listing under Smith Orthodontics, and then another under John Smith, DMD, MS. That's fine ... except one is taking away from the other. So if it were me, I'd eliminate the "John Smith, DMD, MS" listing, so all the 'good' SEO goes to "Smith Orthodontics."

- **Number Three: your web site should be optimized, too**. Every time it goes on a search for "Orthodontists in Anytown," Google's algorithm is looking for specific words in specific places. If your web site designers haven't put those important key words in the right place, the algorithm may rank you lower or skip over your entirely.

There's an easy way to check this at the very top level. Go to Google and type in "Orthodontist in Anytown," and look at your practice when it comes up. If you see a listing that says, "Smith Orthodontics," as you want it to, followed by the address, the phone number, maybe even "braces" and "Invisalign," that's good. If it says, "Home – Smith Orthodontics," and nothing else, or has a wrong address (or no address), or worst of all if it doesn't show up at all, the site is probably not properly optimized, and you need to get that fixed. Your listing has a specific number of characters available, and you should have SEO-enabled title tags right where the algorithm is looking for them.

Concentrate on these areas first when you're looking at how to get into the "three-pack" with your best possible listing. It's not magic, and it's not foolproof; there are many factors that go into how you get found and chosen by potential patients, which is why SEO consultants make so much money and make no guarantees. And by the way: any good SEO company should tell you that. They *shouldn't* make guarantees; the landscape is constantly changing, and every practice and market is different. No one can guarantee you anything, and anybody that does isn't the person or company you want to be dealing with.

So those are the basics for Search Engine Optimization?

Beth: Those are the basics ... but remember, it's not a quick fix. It's an ongoing commitment. Unfortunately, every practice I know gets calls every week – or every day – from SEO 'experts' who say they have the next big thing ... and 90% of them don't. Still, through it all, the basics remain the same: work with a good web site design company from the beginning, and on an ongoing basis to fix some of biggest issues. Get reports regularly. Ask them what they can do for you, and tell them what needs to be done. Most reputable companies are well aware of what the major, current SEO issues are and how to fix them, so it's just a matter of time and resources.

Social media: which ones and how often?

What about social media? You say that Google is looking for "a good online presence." Does that include being on Twitter, Facebook, and other social media?

Beth: It absolutely does. Social media involvement is hugely important to the Google social media.

Which ones matter most?

Beth: There's not one simple answer. The number of social media is infinite and always evolving, though not as quickly as Google algorithms. Be sure to be on the major ones for orthodontic practice growth: Facebook, Twitter, and InstaGram. Remember, 96% of decisions about orthodontic care *for the whole family* are made by women between the ages of 30 and 65, and those women are on Facebook and – more and more -- InstaGram. Twitter matters, too. Some are on SnapChat, though it's not clear if that's beneficial yet; some practices like Pinterest. That's as much a matter of personal preference as anything else. But Facebook, InstaGram, and Twitter are essential.

So how often should a practice be posting? And does time of day matter?

Beth: Most practices I know post once a day, or at least three to five times a week. After a lot of measurement and trial and error, we've found that time of day *does* matter, and even the best post that goes up at the 'wrong' time is wasted. The best times seem to be at the beginning or the end of the day, early morning or late afternoon – 7:00 a.m. to 9:00 a.m. or 5:30 p.m. to 7:30 p.m., when people are getting home and browsing through their social media before dinner. And that *doesn't* mean you have to be online all the time yourself. There are plenty of very good, very cheap (or free!) tools available that can help you write and schedule those posts in advance, and have them released at the best possible time, no matter where or how busy you are.

On-line reviews:
How to get them, how to handle them

One last question, and it's a big one: how important are online reviews, like the ones on Google and Yelp!? And how can a practice generate good ones and avoid bad ones?

Beth: How important are they? *Very* important. That's the simple answer. It's been impressed upon us, especially in the last five years, that they are a major factor in being noticed and attracting new patients.

I don't think any doctor likes having reviews. They don't like asking for them, don't like the fact that people can sit in their waiting area and write a review about them on their phone without even seeing the doctor. It's a challenging scenario, but it's not going to get any better. And it's here to stay

In many ways, reviews are just as important – maybe *more* important – than personal or professional referrals. Let me give you an example from my own life. I have a good friend, someone I've known for a long time, who has given me good recommendations about a lot of things over the years. I trust her, and we have similar tastes in a lot of ways. But some time ago, she recommended a pancake restaurant to me -- a place right down the street. And I *do* trust her, so I didn't check the place out online, didn't read any reviews. I just went … and it was the worst place I've ever eaten in my life. Greasy and disgusting. So after I got out of there, I went on my phone and looked up reviews of that place for the first time, and they were god-awful. Yelp! was right, and my friend was wrong. Now she's still my friend. I still like her and believe her *most* of the time. But I'll never trust her with my food choices again and I will *always* check Yelp! before I go to a new restaurant, no matter who recommends it. That's the power of online reviews.

Which review sites are important has changed over time, too. It's actually become very focused. Not so long ago, there were a number of different review platforms like Angie's List and Yahoo Local Listings, alongside a billion other smaller platforms. Now it's pretty much shaken out to Yelp! and Google, though Facebook and smaller sites like HealthGrades and RateMD are still effective. Yelp! isn't in all areas, but even if the smallest towns where you wouldn't think Yelp! would be a factor, it often is. It's worth taking seriously. All in all: they matter more than you probably think.

So how can an orthodontic practice go about getting as many good reviews as possible?

Beth: You ask exactly the right question: *as many good reviews as possible*. Though high ranking, positive reviews, are very important, obviously, the *number* of reviews is just as important. One of the strongest reasons you get into that three-pack is because you have a *lot* of good reviews.

So how can you make 'a lot of good reviews' happen?

Beth: In this instance, it's not really very different from getting personal or professional referrals: the most important thing you can do is to *ask happy patients to review you on line*. On the other hand, it *is* different from referrals in one important way. Referrals always works best from a doctor, not just a staff member. Reviews are different. Staff members can ask for a review and get it. It's doesn't have to be doctor-driven, but it *does* have to be practice-driven.

The best strategies for getting those good reviews has changed over time. When they first became important, we treated them exactly like referrals; we asked for them when the patients were in the office. "Hey, would you mind doing a review right now? Here's our computer, just put your information in and write a review." In those days, no review site asked where you were doing it – nobody was thinking about IP addresses and such. Today, of course, you have to log in, you have to be on your own device, you have to remember your password and you have to be able to post directly to the system. Because of all that, after a while, the in-office computer station strategy actually started to work against us.

So we tried e-mailing. At the end of each day, all the patients who had visited the office that day would get an e-mail thanking them for coming in and asking them to fill out a short survey about the experience. The patients who gave the highest ratings were then asked if they would mind posting a positive review on their favorite review site.

We got 20% or less to do that. There were a lot of reasons: people don't open their e-mail, or they were happy to go through the survey process with your internal form but wouldn't take it to the next level and post it on Google or wherever. Some practices still try and do it this way, and there have been some improvements over the years, but in my experience, it's rare that a practice gets more than 20-30% of those who write reviews to move them to Google or Yelp!

For a while, we even tried to give out instruction sheets to recent visitors. Treatment Coordinators and others were incentivized to hand out those sheets to show how happy patients could do the reviewing from their phone or home computer. It didn't take long to see that doesn't work. The minute a Mom leaves your office, she's off to a soccer game or ballet practice, there's grocery shopping to do or homework to get started. People are *busy*; they don't have time to worry about what *your* needs are. Capturing them in the office still seemed like the best alternative, but how could we do that?

The almost universal use of the cell phone changed everything. Again. Today, everyone in American has a cell phone. Even my 81-year-old mother knows how to get on to Yelp! and leave a review. So getting them to write a review, right there in the office, is easier than it has been in years. You just have to ask – often and regularly.

But can you get them to write good reviews?

Beth: That's a little tougher. My best advice is to be very careful and selective about who you ask, and when. That's half the battle. Focus on people who are happiest with the practice *at that moment*. In general, patients are happy at the beginning when they're first signed up and committed, happy during the first eight to ten weeks when they see a lot of positive changes -- when the most dramatic changes are visible. They're <u>*not*</u> so super-happy when they've been in braces for eighteen months and they're still six months away from being done. That's not a good time to ask for a review. But at the end of the process, when you unveil that gorgeous smile, they're super-happy again, so that's another time to ask for a review. And there's one more time that's appropriate: when somebody comes up and says, "Oh my gosh, I can't believe how great Johnny's teeth are looking!" or, "Oh my gosh, I love your staff, they're the best, they did XYZ." When somebody pays you a compliment, that's a great time to ask them for a review.

Try texting, too. Ask them directly to log in on their own phone or table or device, and see if that helps. Texting has become very, very effective for many age groups.

They're may be better ways to do this in the future, and the future could be tomorrow, because technology turns on a dime these days. But right now: that's the best scenario for getting good reviews. It's come full circle: we started by asking happy patients in the office, and then that stopped working for a while. Now, we find that asking directly, at the right time, right there in the office, is the best way to go once again … though timing is very important.

I know it's difficult, and I know your team feels that they don't have the time to do this. We're all pushed. But it's a huge part of your practice. Remember, people felt the same way about asking for referrals, and they often still do: "We don't have time." But really, it's not that you don't have time; it's that you don't feel comfortable doing it … and you have to get over that. It's one of the very best ways to grow your practice.

And finally ... what can we do about bad reviews?

Beth: Well, number one: they're inevitable. The best thing you can do is to keep an eye out for them, respond carefully and diplomatically and *quickly* when you see them, and try to resolve the patient's concern. And ask for help from your SEO people or a reputation management expert if you need to. These 'hits' to your reputation can be very damaging. But really, the best way to handle a bad review is with an overwhelming number of *good* reviews. Bury the bad ones with good ones, so they get lost in the shuffle.

So SEO, social media, online reviews ... all of these are important, and not just once in a while, but all the time and from now on.

Beth: Yes.

You know, I've lived in the orthodontic marketing world for the last ten years, and I've had clients tell me, "I don't want to be listed in Yelp; I don't care about Google. Just take me out." But you don't have a choice. Unfortunately, Yelp! and Google aren't optional. If you have a business of any kind – especially an orthodontic practice – you're going to be there, like it or not.

The thing is: it can actually be fun. There are almost certainly people on your team who *love* social media and will be happy to be part of posting on Facebook and InstaGram. And people like hearing compliments about the practice, acknowledgements of their hard work. Spreading the good word can work for you in a lot of ways. But bottom line: the internet and social media are here to stay, so you might as well accept it ... and you'll probably even learn to enjoy it.

Thanks, Beth!

Anyone interested in Beth Leach and what she can do for your practice should contact her at

wwwPracticeMarketer.com

Chapter 6

Endgame

Tracking, Testing, and Taking Care of the Team

So the research has been done, the plan's been made. The doctor (or doctors) are on board, and the team is ready.

Just a few more words and you're ready to get started!

Tracking and Rewarding

Don't let all your hard work fade away. Yes, practice growth is a never-ending process, but part of that process is measuring what's worked (and what hasn't), so you can build on the best ideas and reward the people who make the whole enterprise successful.

First and most important: every promotion, *every single one*, should have a tracking code or symbol. You should know how every patient who comes in the door first heard about you, why they chose you, and how often they will be returning.

Your patient management software can be a lot of help – probably more than you know. Look into what tracking and reporting it can do for you, and add checking those reports to your regular calendar.

In my practice, we track:

- The source of every new patient (how they found us)
- Every patient's dentist
- Referrals from that patient (number of referrals, date and name)

… as well as all the procedures, family members, strategic dates and contact information we talked about earlier.

Then, at the end of every month I run the report that gives me a list of who my leading professional and patient referrers were, and how well my other promotional events went, since all of them have individual source codes as well. It gets *trend information* out of this, too, that tells me how productive all of this month's activity was compared to last month's, to the year so far, to the same period of time last year, as well as *rewards information*, so I know who to thank for their help, who deserves the investment of more time and attention as a 'practice builder,' and what promotions need to be improved, repeated or – occasionally – abandoned.

It's worth noting: *all* information, even the disappointing data, are important to know. Finding out what you did right is great, but it's equally important to know what went wrong, so you can avoid repeating those mistakes or building on failure. You're absolutely allowed to be disappointed if a team member or promotional events doesn't live up to expectations, for whatever reason, but please: try not to take it personally. You can exhaust yourself that way.

Then turn your attention to that rewards information. It's gold.

The tried-and-true rewards – tickets to sporting events,

gift certificates for Starbucks, Amazon, or popular local stores, restaurant passes – are tried-and-true for a reason: people respond well to them and always have. But we're always on the look-out for new rewards as well, innovations that not only thank the people who deserve to be thanked, but to get them talking about the cool thing our practice did for them. After all, why not turn your rewards system into a promotional campaign of its own?

Timing of the rewards are important as well. If it's someone new – someone who hasn't referred before -- the minute they come in we respond in person, rewarding them right there, so they know we appreciate them sending a patient our way. We send cards in the mail as well – gifts cards to places like Starbucks or Panera, that are almost always appreciated, thanking them for referring the friend. We even had a special card made for that program – our "Thanks a Latte" card that includes a $10 Starbucks gift card. You can see the front and back on the next page.

And don't underestimate the power of the personal. Thank you cards are always signed by a real person, not "The Practice" or "The Team." In the case of our practice that's *me*, because I'm the one who's in there, I'm the one who's doing the job and doing the tracking. But whoever's name you choose to put on the card, remember: the power of that personal relationship is huge. If you go from being "just a business" – even one your patient likes and admires – to an actual *person*, the chances that they will recommend you again – and over and over -- go way, way up. The proven path to a great ROI is simply saying "thank you" in the most memorable way you can.

One last word about tracking codes, too: *get creative*. They don't have to be complicated alphanumeric system. In fact, it's better if they aren't. Even though every one of my discount cards has some sort of code for the event or promotion involved, we make them both invisible and clever at the same time by using unique symbols when we can. The little symbol for cards given out on the Fourth of July is fireworks. One year all the cards for school promotions shows the Pink Panther in the corner, along with some other symbol so we could tell one school from another. And of course, we maintain a master list of all the symbols, no matter how old, that anyone who's working at the front desk or opening the mail can access.

Which reminds me: *never put expiration dates on any promotion*. Even if they come in a year or two later, they are always welcome in our practice. Why wouldn't they be? It gives us valuable information along with a new patient. And we know that Moms (and others) hang on to those cards, and when the time comes, they respond. It's not surprising to see a discount card from an event or a school visit come in from one or two years in the past – or even older. So *no expiration dates*. It's counter-productive.

Keep trying new things, keep testing the "standards"

The old cliché is absolutely true: the only thing that stays the same is *change*. And though some events and promotions work every year, almost like clockwork, others outlive their usefulness, while other new opportunities are always popping up.

Every year, I try to add something new to the plan

– usually *more* than one thing – just to keep current. You have to say up with the times; you can't do the same thing every year, over and over again, as easy (and inviting!) as that would be. Of course, you're going to attend that same successful and popular community events every year, but the last thing you want to hear is, "Oh, look, there's Mel again." If you're that familiar, you're *predictable*, and they're not going to respond. So we're always trying, measuring and refining as we test something new: New contests, new internet promotions, new give-aways. We even change the signage at our both to keep it eye-catching – to *make* potential patients come to see us and even seek us out.

Here's just one example. This year, for that big community event, I had the idea of a "Make Your Own Ortho Smile" booth. So we bought a few dozen big, beautiful cookies in various flavors from a popular local bakery and set them out alongside plenty of frosting and cake-decoration goodies, so that anyone who came by our booth could make their own "smiley-face" cookie for free. They left with a funny and tasty desert, a practice brochure *and* a (coded) discount card. It was a hit … and all I know for sure is a year or two from now, it will be replaced by an even bigger hit.

So keep changing. Keep trying new things. Keep testing, adjusting, and moving on. Don't give anyone the opportunity to get bored.

The Calendar is Your Friend

If you've done the job you need to do in planning,

you have a marketing and promotional calendar for the year already done, whether it's in a notebook, on a computer, or online. You can use that calendar for team-building and motivation, as well as employ it as a valuable communications tool.

Add a new bulletin board (or commandeer an underused one) in your break room or staff lounge. Put up a colorful version of your Calendar that covers the next twelve months, with plenty of details for what's coming up in the next three months. But *do* have it stretch a full year into the future, because many people plan that far out. Make a commitment to bring it up to date every quarter or so, so it's always looking twelve months into the future.

Use that board to stay organized, build anticipation, and acknowledge success and commitment. Make sure everything's written out for the immediate future – vacations, days out, community events, birthdays and holidays, all of it. And pin up pictures or thank-you notes from recent events that went very well. It's amazing how something so simple can bring people together and keep everyone faced in the same direction: towards success.

Reward your team like you reward your referrers

You already know how a rewards program can work wonders for professional and personal referrals. Keep in mind that rewards and acknowledgements can work just as well – maybe even better! – with the members of your own team.

We work hard and consistently to make sure our own team members feel appreciated, even in small ways. There's a "Reward Jar" in the lounge that gets presented at a meeting every month – a little thing like mints or munchies, awarded to someone who went the extra mile. And we make sure it doesn't seem rushed or incidental. For instance, I recently drew up a label for a Rewards Jar that read, "Thanks for the EXTRA Effort," and filled to the brim with *Extra* Sugar-Free Gum, just to make it something special. It was a hit.

We have a permanent Gratitude Board in the lounge as well, and I'm happy to report I'm not the only one who keeps it current. Whenever anyone goes above and beyond, messages "magically" appear on the board, thanking them for what they did in a public way. The notes and "thank you's" get noticed, and the message is clear even if you're not the one being thanked: *you matter*. Little things like this can turn a happy office into a *successful* office, and that makes everyone happier.

And remember: almost everything you're asking of your team is *voluntary*. You can't force them to be part of your growth team; they have to *want* to do it. And believe me, success rates go way down if you try to make it mandatory.

We include everyone. We make it fun, rather than required. We say, "We'd love to have you," and we talk with genuine excitement and pride about what's working and what we're doing next. If a new member of the staff doesn't want to be involved, we don't push it. We know if they don't enjoy it, they won't do a good job. But when we all come back after a big weekend event, the new arrival sees all the gratitude being offered to those who helped out; they hear about what a great time everyone had and laugh at all the stories. After that, they almost always *want* to join in next time – to be part of it. They feel part of the process and valued.

This is something worth thinking about when you hire new people, too. Show them the Calendar on the wall in the lounge when you're giving the grand tour and take note of how they respond. Make it clear that participation in the team is part of the commitment, not just something mentioned in the employee handbook. What you're looking for in a new employee is an individual who's ready and even eager to take that on, and if you see any doubts, any "I don't know if I want to do this," then maybe they're not the right person to bring into the practice. Especially if they're part of the "front office" team, you have to make sure that they are 150% behind the practice and the plan, and that they're committed to growth and improvement, inside and out.

Once you find the right people for the right job ... the rest is easy.

Final Words:
You're One of a Kind. Celebrate it!

I've covered a lot of the basics in this book – things that have worked for my home practice and for the many practices I've worked with. And I know, much of the time I'm speaking in generalities. That's the nature of the business.

The fact is, there's no one book you can read or webinar you can watch that's going to give you "the secret." Different things work for different practices in different markets. That's why we put some much emphasis "up front" on learning as much as you can about your doctor, you team, or organization, and your community: so you can start to build an effective and *individual* plan for growth.

Every single practice is different. None are identical. And that's a good thing, as challenging as it can be sometimes. The plan you build and execute – and keep changing and improving all the time – it is *yours*, and nobody else's.

You can learn from other people's success, and I hope some of the tips and tactics I've talked about here can help with that, but really, the success of your plan and practice will be based in large part on *who you are*, what makes you unique. In the end, there's no secret recipe … but there are a lot of great ingredients that can work for you as they have for so many other people. Don't be frustrated by that. *Celebrate it.* Set yourself apart. And know that what you're doing, now in in the months to come, is right for you, your team, and your practice … and no one else.

You're special. Act like it!

Time to get to work!

Melissa Herbinko

Melissa Herbinko began her career in 1991. She is the office liaison to area dentists and the public for a large multi-doctor practice in the Midwest, charged with fostering strong relationships with referring dentists and their staff. She makes visits to local schools, helping to educate children on orthodontics and oral health. Melissa participates in community events, answering questions about orthodontic care while promoting the benefits of orthodontic treatment.

Contact Melissa at melherbinko@gmail.com

www.ingramcontent.com/pod-product-compliance
Lightning Source LLC
Chambersburg PA
CBHW071603220526
45469CB00003B/1102